True Greatness

Let's go be
Great - From

New York Life

/w
68

True Greatness

*Mastering the Inner Game
of Business Success*

Kevin Elko and Bill Beausay

⁄AMACOM

American Management Association

New York • Atlanta • Brussels • Chicago • Mexico City • San Francisco
Shanghai • Tokyo • Toronto • Washington, D.C.

Special discounts on bulk quantities of AMACOM books are available to corporations, professional associations, and other organizations. For details, contact Special Sales Department, AMACOM, a division of American Management Association, 1601 Broadway, New York, NY 10019.
Tel: 212-903-8316. Fax: 212-903-8083.
E-mail: specialsls@amanet.org
Website: www.amacombooks.org/go/specialsales
To view all AMACOM titles go to: www.amacombooks.org

This publication is designed to provide accurate and authoritative information in regard to the subject matter covered. It is sold with the understanding that the publisher is not engaged in rendering legal, accounting, or other professional service. If legal advice or other expert assistance is required, the services of a competent professional person should be sought.

Library of Congress Cataloging-in-Publication Data

Elko, Kevin
    True greatness : mastering the inner game of business success / Kevin Elko and Bill Beausay.
        p.   cm.
    Includes bibliographical references and index.
    ISBN-13: 978-0-8144-1301-2
    ISBN-10: 0-8144-1301-3
    1. Success in business.   2. Success.   3. Conduct of life.   I. Title.
HF5386.E39   2009
650.1—dc22

                                                    2009002130

Printing Number

10   9   8   7   6   5   4   3

Contents

Introduction

A funny story is told of a retired greyhound who was interviewed by a newspaper reporter following his sudden and unexpected retirement. He was asked whether he considered his career to be a success.

"Very successful," he replied matter-of-factly.

"Did you win any money?" asked the reporter.

"Over $5 million for my owner," replied the greyhound nonchalantly. "And I had several very successful offspring as well."

"Did you suffer any injuries?"

"No," he replied with the confidence of a champion.

"Why, then, are you retiring?"

The greyhound stared off for a moment, then answered. "I found out the rabbit I was chasing around the track wasn't real."

We have learned so much in our study of greatness. Chief among those lessons is that we all chase rabbits throughout our lives. This chase leads to vague feelings of frustration and unhappiness. It also leads us far away from anything approaching what we'd define as a better way to live. Living a better life simply gets lost in the daily race. None of us wants to live chasing imaginary rabbits.

But what do any of us really know about living our lives on a higher plateau? How can we take hold of a better way of life that we vaguely sense is possible when we're so burdened by the day-in, day-out rabbit chase? How can we live and work in a way that brings not only more financial and career success, but also a deeper and more meaningful real-life satisfaction at the same time?

True greatness is living life on a higher plateau than just counting possessions, achievements, accolades, and goals. Those, as it turns out, are fake rabbits. True greatness happens when your life is centered on the deeper concerns of life that we all share, like finding peace and experiencing satisfaction with ourselves. True greatness is about making choices from an out-of-the-ordinary mindset and about having the feeling that your life is getting some meaningful and satisfying traction in the right direction. True greatness is about living a life filled with joy, passion, success, excitement, and peace.

Everyone is always fascinated by the person who in midlife decides to quit his job and go work at a mission in India. Or the person who cashes in all her insurance and investments and starts a nonprofit project to buy shoes for Brazilian orphans. Or the person, like Paul Newman, Oprah, Bill Gates, and others, who after experiencing great life success decides to invest much of his or her time helping underprivileged people get a life worth living. All these people (and thousands like them) decided that their lives were about more than just *accumulation*. Life began feeling pointless to them, and they took action, often in a radically different direction.

True greatness is about seeking a special kind of "more" in life. It's not about gathering and keeping a staggering amount of money or possessions, though there's nothing intrinsically wrong with that, but about having a profound sense of personal self-worth, worthwhileness, and a satisfaction that goes beyond material things.

This kind of greatness, true greatness, is a soft, urgent, calling within nearly all of us. You've certainly felt it: that magical *something* within you, urging you to live from a different and more meaningful place. It's the subtle, practically transcendent urge to be a better person, to give rather than take, to forgive and be kind, and so on. "The biggest human temptation is to settle for too little" said the famed philosopher and theologian Thomas Merton. He was referring to chasing rabbits: settling for less than joy, the fruits of great character, passion, excitement, and the thrill of exercising our unique calling in life. He was observing that most people simply settle for something less than true greatness. It's our goal to help you aim at *that* higher plateau of life and never again to settle for simply counting possessions as a means of feeling success.

We hope that you recognize this calling within yourself and push yourself to pursue the simple path to true richness we describe in this book. We believe that not only will you discover more real world riches and success along the path, but that you can avoid the greyhound's dilemma, and begin experiencing a new kind of life that you can truly fall in love with.

True Greatness

CHAPTER 1

Are You Scripted for True Greatness?

There is nothing more difficult to take in hand,
more perilous to conduct,
or more uncertain in its success,
than to take the lead
in the introduction of a new order to things.

NICCOLO MACHIAVELLI

With the publication of *True Greatness*, we hope to generate something special for you, something like the terrific results we get when working with athletes. That means activating your inner desire to take action and to make tangible change at deep levels. It also means creating a new way of thinking about greatness.

True greatness comes *when you activate that deep motivation* existing in the heart of nearly everyone—you included. That motivation presses you to seek worthwhile pursuits, usefulness, meaning beyond the ordinary. It represents one of the most profoundly good motivations a human being can experience.

1

If you're reading this book, you have a strong desire to better yourself. That's good because this book is your opportunity to get that feeling to rise within you. But trust us on one thing: This book is not a one-way street where we talk and you just listen. You have a major part in this play. We can't simply teach and expect good things just to appear. This effort won't do any good without you. In the hands of a casual reader or a skeptic, this information will fall flatter than a cracker. Yet an open-minded reader can create a huge leap in lifestyle, success, and personal satisfaction.

Your personal motivation for wanting to change is hugely important in how you learn and use this information. To figure out why you want to improve yourself, look at your life scripts. Most behavior (particularly dysfunctional behavior) is learned as a result of conscious choices made over and over for the purpose of survival. Such choices culminate in beliefs that solidify in what are called "life scripts." These life scripts get so deep in us that they are barely conscious. They govern what you believe and how you live. They represent a general attitude or orientation on which you base most decisions, perceptions, and choices.

There are many possible scripts, functional and dysfunctional, such as:

- I will always protect myself at any cost.
- My life is mine to be lived any way I choose.
- I am smarter than everyone, and I will prove it.

- I am a piece of garbage who deserves nothing.

- Life is not about creation; life is about doing what you're told.

- If I expose who I really am, people won't like me.

- The only way to protect myself is to attack.

- It is better to be right than to grow.

- My life is about serving others.

- If I am nice enough, everyone will love me.

- I can take something from this experience that will make me great.

- And on and on . . .

These scripts (and you might have several) constitute a mental organizing principle for making choices in life, and they deeply affect your inner urge for true greatness. To that end, they can help you or they can disable your efforts. Let's look at two different life scripts that came out of two very similar sets of experiences and how they affected their owners' reach for true greatness.

Consider the story of Sally, a woman who had been sexually abused as a teenager. The abuse was offensive and the mental anguish extensive. This woman had made a decision based on her experience never to trust men again or give them the opportunity to become close to her. She effectively committed her life to avoiding men and never revealing any hint of emotional need or desire. She had repeated this decision to herself over and over to the point where she no longer was even aware that her life was scripted for loneliness. Her script was not for transcendent happiness, but rather for safety and isolation.

Now consider the story of Clara Barton, founder of the Red Cross. She was once asked about a similar circumstance in her life where she was repeatedly wronged by another person. It was a very costly type of abuse and difficult to get past. When she was asked about it, Clara Barton said simply that she didn't remember it. "In fact," she went on, "I distinctly remember forgetting it."

This life script directed Barton to handle her relationships and her life in a forward looking, hopeful way, not backward looking and angry. When things weren't going well, her script directed her to keep pressing ahead. Her script urged her to move on without dwelling on past anguish. This script allowed her to find a place of greater inner peace instead of a place of anger and bitterness.

To see true greatness in your life, you need scripts that permit it. Greatness scripts are those that open you, not close you. They allow for open-minded exploration in the face of problems, as well as the creative application of problem-solving strategies, rather than harsh hostile reactions that cause your attitude to spiral into negativity. For example, a script that assists you in your pursuit of true greatness in your career directs you to focus calmly on finding joy in your work circumstances. A script that deflects you from true greatness in your career directs you to second-guess yourself and your ability to feel good about the things you do in your work.

You even bring a script to the primary task of this book: You are filtering what you read through your scripts and making decisions about how you feel inside. Do not allow *any* scripts to run inside you without noticing them and challenging them, if necessary. Are your natural reactions to situations helping you or harming you? Challenging the scripts that are working against true greatness begins by becoming aware of yourself and noticing your natural thoughts and emotional reactions to difficult situations. Be honest with yourself about what you see. Start by taking a small amount of time to check yourself: Strive to be open-minded to challenging and improving yourself. Most people aren't automatically scripted to move to a place of greatness, much less have experience in manifesting greatness. They've just chased rabbits too long and won't give up the chase. And let's face it: The pursuit of true inner peace and contentment can get frustrating. True greatness, as it turns out, has a two-sided nature: It is both easy to bring out, yet tricky. It is easy because all the elements are in all of us, yet it is tricky because our lives are full of competing scripts, noise, busyness, and an endless array of both conscious and unconscious distractions. When people are over-burdened, their conscious attention narrows to the things that are the most important to survival. Manifesting greatness loses out to participating in countless other mental and physical distractions.

Take the time to monitor how you automatically react to

new opportunities. Set yourself about the task of allowing your inner life scripts for greatness to emerge and function fully in your minute-by-minute attitudes. Speak to yourself in ways that foster inner greatness, and be careful about addressing old attitudes and behaviors that would stop your ascent to true greatness before you've even begun.

Choosing to follow that inner path honestly to true satisfaction despite the challenges is being scripted for greatness.

You can liberate yourself from the grind of routine mediocrity and build life scripts for true greatness. Don't let everyday obligations stop you. It really isn't that hard to learn.

Once you begin to have a sense of how you are scripted now and have made a determined decision to change whatever is necessary, you're ready to take on the next challenge.

The Next Challenge

That challenge is seeing clearly where you are going and getting a clear vision of true greatness. One of the leading causes of failure in the pursuit of anything is simply the lack of a clear idea of where you're aiming your energy. What does true greatness look like? What is the target at which you must aim yourself to be successful in hitting it? How do you acquire a vision that will take you where you want to go?

CHAPTER 2

The Joy of Being Something and Knowing That You Are Advancing

---∞---

Great men are they who see that
spiritual is stronger than material force,
that thoughts rule the world.

RALPH WALDO EMERSON

---∞---

Truly successful athletes and business leaders are successful in their minds long before they ever reach the gridiron or the boardroom. They have discovered the power of controlling their own minds and owning their vision. Interestingly, this is the path to true greatness as well. How do you acquire this sort of transcendent greatness using your mind and your focus? The answer is surprisingly simple, and it's not what you'd think. This chapter defines the exact attributes of creating true greatness first in your mind and gives you a specific target at which to aim your energy. It begins with knowing the difference between excellence and true greatness.

Excellence Versus Greatness

As a practical matter, you must understand the difference between excellence and greatness. *Excellence* is the process of taking some personal talent or skill and stretching it as far as it can go. It could take the form of rigorous training to break a world record or studying to get straight As. This is excellence: developing your talents as far as possible. Excellence is a wonderful thing and is what most people think of when they think of greatness.

True *greatness*, however, is not an extension of excellence; it is an entirely different game. It is not attainable through training and straining and working yourself physically. True greatness is about living life from a core belief that says you don't accumulate or compete yourself to personal happiness, but pursue it for inner motivations. We like the words of Wallace Wattles in his classic book, *The Science of Being Great*, as he describes the pursuit of greatness:

> Great people never seek for recognition or applause; they are not great because they want to be paid for being so. Greatness is reward enough for itself; *the joy of being something and of knowing that you are advancing* is the greatest of all joys possible to man.

There is a curious, almost mysterious truth in the words of Wallace Wattles. His words tempt us to think deeper about the nature of pursuing true greatness. How do we find the "joy of being something and knowing you are advancing"?

Let's start with what we know about true greatness:

- Greatness is rare.

- Greatness is a process that starts in your head.

- Greatness needs to be exercised.

- Greatness is possible for anyone.

- Greatness is social.

- Greatness is selfless.

Greatness Is Rare

True greatness has an unmistakable beyond-the-ordinary feeling to it. You *know* something unusual or perhaps profound is happening when you encounter it. You can simply sense that you are in the presence of someone special. If you think back to all the people you have known in your life, you can think of a small handful who stood out in this way. Perhaps they demonstrated some unusual act of leadership or kindness that was timely and unique, perhaps they did something special or remarkable, or maybe they just touched you in a special way. It's interesting—don't you think—how three or four people can just stay in your memory like that? The experience of encountering greatness is rare.

Greatness Is a Process
That Starts in Your Head

Greatness is not magic. It begins within the six inches between your ears. If one person can do it, anyone can. Though few choose greatness, life seems to offer endless opportunities, almost minute by minute, to do something truly great. But only great minds see those opportunities and act accordingly. You will begin seeing them soon. It's a sign you are learning.

Greatness Needs to Be Exercised

So much of life is automatic. We can literally live great chunks of our lives in autopilot mode, simply going through the motions of existence. Greatness never grows from a mind drifting in this fashion. Greatness is a deliberate act—thoughtful, prepared, rehearsed, exercised, and displayed.

Greatness Is Possible for Anyone

Greatness is not about intelligence, talent, motivation, personality, or fads. In fact, greatness has nothing to do with intelligence at all. Great people are not a breed apart. If you had known Martin Luther King Jr. or Albert Schweitzer in school, you probably would not have thought of either as particularly amazing or smart or special. But certain qualities about them would emerge. These qualities would include sharing, encouraging, ego-lessness, optimism, thoughtfulness, curiosity, courage, leadership, and so on. These qualities, though unique, are not in the DNA. They are simply human traits that individuals—any individuals—choose to exercise and develop. Great people choose to display these traits consistently over time. In hindsight it's clear that these qualities, openly shared, are what set these people apart. They started out just like everyone else, but choosing to develop different personal traits. Greatness is an open game, available to anyone.

Greatness Is Social

Greatness is linked to *interpersonal* events, not just to personal achievement. Loners report lower levels of self-satisfaction in almost all categories measured. Dwelling on happy, thankful thoughts toward others for a half hour a day will generate significant changes in optimism and purpose in just two weeks. Greatness has a strong social element.

Greatness Is Selfless

Selflessness means taking action in life for reasons that are beyond yourself. How do you do this? When you study the words of mankind's great teachers and philosophers on the topic of greatness, you will find that there is huge overlap among them at one very crucial and interesting spot: the need to *give up your personal agenda to benefit others.*

There may be a biological root to this. Brain science suggests that the rudiments of greatness are present in all human beings. Healthy brains have a good supply of a neurotransmitter called serotonin. It is called the "happy hormone" because people who have high levels of serotonin in their brains are happy and upbeat. Serotonin is missing or low in people who are depressed all the time. Many antidepressant medications work simply by raising the serotonin levels in the brain.

When you do something heroic or courageous—that is, selfless—serotonin is released into your bloodstream in large quantities. Your body reacts to the experience of greatness by releasing chemicals to make you feel good; this is a biological means of rewarding behavior and encouraging its reoccurrence. But get this: If you receive or even just observe a kind act, serotonin levels go crazy high in your brain too. What's happening is that your brain is recognizing goodness and making you feel good in response. It's amazing, really. Simply witnessing a great business deal close, hearing a motivational speech, watching someone win a gold medal, witnessing an act of kindness, and so on actually makes you feel great.

For some reason, we're programmed to recognize and respond to acts of greatness with some sense of feel-good. It's biological: It's as if your body is naturally rewarding you for something it wants you to repeat. Interestingly, serotonin levels do not go up when people experience personal power, acquiring security or fulfilling desires, or any of the other traditional definitions of happiness, success, and excellence. We are clearly not programmed for selfish forms of success by itself. What many people think will make them happy, in truth, does not.

This biological facts are borne out in real life. There is story after story about people giving up their own needs so that others may benefit. The entire *Chicken Soup for the Soul* franchise was built on stories of ordinary folks who exercised greatness simply by giving up their own selfish needs to help others. Something about those stories stirs us. They have the mark of rightness about them. It's as if there is a universal knowing that to be selfless is rare and worth doing.

Yet despite this knowing, we have not traditionally been taught that selflessness is the best way to succeed. Instead we have been indoctrinated to think that the only way to get ahead is by tirelessly competing, selling, persuading, fighting, worrying, pressuring, cajoling, and so on. We've been taught that selfishness is how you get the things that make you happy. Right?

Well, not really. It appears that true greatness may have less to do with making yourself happy and more about making others benefit from what you bring to the world.

Let's boil this down: True greatness is finding that special inner place of peace, purpose, and happiness that is of a different order than material achievement. You find the path to this place by developing your gift or gifts and using them to serve some purpose beyond just yourself, day in and day out. You can live a life that transcends your individual existence. You can make a difference.

—⚬—

Hide not your talent, they for use were made.
What's a sundial in the shade?

Ben Franklin

—⚬—

A Pure Example of True Greatness: Golda Meir

The elements of true greatness are hiding in plain sight. Golda Meir was the prime minister of Israel and widely regarded as one of the true heroes of the 20th century. She was born in Milwaukee, Wisconsin, of immigrant Russian Jewish parents. She was a sensitive, strong, and intelligent girl, committed to her education and to a desire to be a teacher. Though she was married at 19 and taught school, she was consumed with a burden to help the Jewish people of Palestine. She subsequently quit her dream teaching job and canvassed the United States, raising funds to help. Her marriage suffered, ending in divorce, but she was consumed with something she considered a higher calling.

She emigrated to Palestine in her early twenties to live and work on a kibbutz. Tireless behind-the-scenes work damaged her health, but in 1948 her bigger dream came true: The country of Israel was born.

She went back and forth to America several times over the

next few decades, serving selflessly behind the scenes on behalf
of the new Israeli government. Against her personal inclinations,
she became actively involved in the politics of the country in the
1950s. It was a choice motivated not by ego, but by a selfless
desire to see something great happen for Israel, no matter what
the personal cost to her. And the personal cost was great: She was
diagnosed with lymphoma in the early 1960s and would quietly
fight cancer the rest of her days.

In the late 1960s, despite failing health and the ravages of
cancer, she was chosen to lead her country as prime minister.
This happened just prior to the surprise 1971 Yom Kippur War
that nearly saw her small country overrun by vastly superior
Egyptian and Syrian forces, as well as the disastrous 1972 Munich
Olympics that saw seven Israeli athletes murdered by terrorists.
She served bravely and successfully. The world might look very
different today if not for her sacrifice.

When Golda went to Palestine as a girl, she was acting *not*
from a mindset or core of "me," but from the core of "others."
She had a powerful and pervasive sense of taking care of others,
even at her own expense, safety, and inconvenience. That is an
entirely unique platform from which to conduct a life. Nobody
is born doing that sort of thing; it is a conscious choice to get
away from the me–me–me that so commonly defines the core of
most people.

Golda Meir's life is a testament to the world-changing power
of seeking true greatness; it is a life that is measured by a better
yardstick than mere personal gain.

Are You Ready?

So now you know what true greatness is and what it involves, and you are ready to upgrade your life.

In the chapters to come, you will learn about a simple five-step path to creating a new inner core of true greatness. Your old thoughts and expectations involved seeing *external* rewards like power, wealth, approval, social advancement, and material things as ways to create *inner* peace and happiness. This is a common and false path. We can all think of major celebrities who at the height of their fame and success became depressed and chose to end their lives. Looking for internal happiness by chasing an external dream is a catastrophic error. An external chase yields little more than frustration and galling emptiness.

The path of true greatness is the total reverse: It is an internal change first that manifests externally second. Inside out.

We hope you will spot greatness hiding within yourself and reach for it eagerly. It is the sure path to true greatness.

In the Quincy Market Holocaust memorial in downtown Boston, six pillars are inscribed with stories of Holocaust survivors. On the sixth pillar, however, is a very different kind of story. It is about a little six-year-old girl named Ilse, friend of Guerda Weisman Kline, an Auschwitz survivor. Guerda recalls that one day little Ilse found a single raspberry somewhere in the camp. Ilse carried it all day long in her pocket, carefully protecting it from damage. That night, she presented it to her friend Guerda on a single leaf. "Imagine a world," wrote Guerda on the pillar, "in which your entire possession is one raspberry, and you give it to your friend." Ilse did a great thing that day, and her sole motivation was to see the smile in her friend's eyes.

———

There are no great things,
only small things done with great love.
Happy are those.

MOTHER TERESA

———

CHAPTER 3

The New Path to True Greatness

While many readers will consciously endorse the lessons of this book, subconsciously they are living by a very different set of rules. Conscious-versus-subconscious misalignment is often the difference between business and life greatness and frustrating failure.

It is important to draw a clear line between what you know on a conscious level and what you truly act on subconsciously. Realigning these two mental levels launches all sorts of new, powerful, and purposeful behavior. It releases intentionality. Influencing your subconscious thinking is your best hope to reveal the greatness hiding within you.

The Perplexed and the Knowing

We like to separate people into two groups: the perplexed and the knowing. Many professional people are doing what they've been told to do to reach success, yet a sense of success eludes them. They've worked toward a life that has the appearance and trappings of success, but a true sense of success slips past them. In their hearts they are quietly wandering, seeking something more deeply satisfying. They are the perplexed.

As it turns out, the standard pathway to success creates something other than reliable peace and power. What it creates looks a lot more like an unquenchable reliance on external rewards for internal satisfaction. This is a mindset that leaves you feeling hollow and desperate for something lasting and sustaining. Those who follow this external path (most of us) end up living in a strange sort of emptiness that is far from our original goal. We're privately frustrated and *perplexed* because we bought into an external system of success, and it has failed us.

Yet other people are *knowing*: They possess something distinctly different deep down inside and are living reflections of those ineffable inner qualities of peace, joy, and happiness, which define a deeper sense of life success. These people don't consciously force their lives to fit together but experience a more graceful and effortless way of living directed by something clear and well aligned *within themselves.*

This internal standard is unshakable. They are rarely slaves to their environment, or battered by the waves of life. Rather they are directed by something deep within. They live from a core that says, "Live in the world, but be not *of* the world." This internal instead of external focus is the source of knowing and of true personal power.

We need to create an *internal* environment so clear, so well ensconced, and so powerful that it literally flows toward the *out-*

side in the form of behavior. Then we need to create a means to protect that inner environment so that it continues to produce fully aligned business habits, people skills, persuasion and negotiation skills, sales ability, and other positive attributes.

We're talking about a vibrant inner mental structure that is not born from simple inspiration or motivation. Inspiration and motivation come from the outside and are like deodorant; eventually they wear off. When inspiration and motivation wear off, you start to stink and need another bath. Rather, we are aiming at making a mental shift that ushers you to true greatness by manifesting happiness from the inside out. That sort of happiness doesn't wear off. Generating happiness from inner resources is crucial for achieving true greatness.

An Age-Old Struggle

The path to deep personal change has never been easy. Cicero (106–43 BCE), the Roman orator, philosopher, and statesman, wrote what he considered to be the top six mistakes made by human beings:

1. The delusion that personal gain is made by crushing others.

2. The tendency to worry about things that cannot be changed.

3. Insisting that something is impossible because we cannot seem to accomplish it.

4. Refusing to set aside trivial preferences.

5. Neglecting development and refinement of the mind, and not acquiring the habit of reading and study.

6. Attempting to compel others to think and live as we do.

These observations are as fresh today as they were 2,000 years ago. Many suffer the same mistakes observed by Cicero. The reality is that mankind hasn't changed all that much over the years, *even when we are shown a clearly better way.* And those who do change themselves have worked very hard to make the changes align both inwardly and outwardly.

Successfully dealing with our own difficult and divided nature is an important task. To successfully make true greatness pervasive and automatic in your life, let's take a closer look at the fundamental structure of the mind.

The Conscious and Subconscious Elements of Greatness

True greatness has a major and a minor premise. The major premise is that the path to it *can be found by selflessly contributing your gifts* and that the highest levels of life fulfillment come to those who will put others ahead of themselves. It is only by going down that narrow path of letting go of your ego and putting others ahead that you can achieve selflessness and higher levels of success. We need to find out specifically how that's done.

The minor premise is no less powerful: Though many people accept the first premise and see that inner peace comes through setting yourself aside and putting others first, very few know it *subconsciously*. In other words, they talk a good game, but the necessary action fails to show up in their daily lives. It's a mismatch between what they *consciously* say they believe and what they really subconsciously believe. To be brutally candid, that incongruence is a huge contributing factor to their failures to find a long-term sense of meaning and purpose.

What Is the Subconscious?

The common conception of the subconscious is a vast and spooky unknown. Sigmund Freud proposed this a century ago to explain many of the darker elements of our behavior, such as our errant thoughts, fantasies, desires, and the like. The modern cognitive psychological view is quite different. Today, the unconscious refers to brain functioning happening outside our awareness. In reality, it's been known for centuries that people act without thinking in many ways and that cognitive processes go on all the time without our immediate awareness. There are countless examples of this: We shower and thoughtlessly go through a morning routine, and we have automatic reactions of all types: day dreaming, sudden unexplained thoughts, anxieties and pleasures, unexplained urges, intuitions, premonitions, surprising yourself, saying things you know better than to say, doing things you don't mean to do but do anyway, and so on. The list of so-called unexplained occurrences in our lives is huge, and there is much more going on in your head than you think. An executive function is running things for you, inside your mind but outside your awareness. What you are actually thinking about consciously (even right now) is a very small fraction of all that is happening in your head.

So our definition of the subconscious is simple: We are referring to that executive mind function that is running many of the details of your life outside your constant awareness and direct observation. If you choose, you can consciously take over and run these processes anytime you want. But for the most part these processes are autonomous and do a pretty good job of running your life.

However, the subconscious element of "you" is susceptible to influence. It can be reached and it can be changed. Let us explain. Several decades ago B. F. Skinner, the single most influential psychologist of the 20th century, wrote a deeply controversial and paradigm shifting book called *Beyond Freedom and Dignity.* In it he stated his belief that, although we imagine differently, we really do not have freedom or dignity (or autonomy to make many choices) in this world. In a sense we don't really make free choices, but rather, without our awareness, life corrals us down certain paths like cattle, and we make the only choices it conditions us (i.e., teaches us) to make. This lack of freedom (as well as subsequently our dignity) is the cause for many of the world's problems, including entire nations hating one another and entire generations of people feeling uncertain, confused, and fearful without the faintest clue why. Because we've been conditioned subconsciously from the outside, we sense a vague and almost unexplainable misalignment with ourselves. It's our minds' way of telling us something is wrong.

Skinner had a good point. How else could our country be so addicted to, say, food and sexuality? Did we choose to be so bloated and obsessed? It can't all be due to biological needs. The reality is that we've been subconsciously conditioned to desire food and physical stimulation in every advertisement on TV, radio, billboard, and newspaper ad we see. We are further force-fed emotionally charged news, music, movies, and negative info-tainment for the sole purpose of conditioning (training) our subconscious minds to buy products.

This subconscious molding is all taking place beyond our awareness. The problem is that there is often a gap, a misalignment between our conscious desire for greatness and our subconsciously molded patterns. The desire and our patterns exist simultaneously and compete with one other. Eventually the gap creates enough discomfort to emerge as anger in our deepest parts. In many ways, this deep-seated discomfort is responsible for fueling poor self-esteem and low self-worth. We really shouldn't be surprised at the general lack of self-esteem and self-respect in this country when every single commercial, sales pitch, and other attempt to mold our minds is telling us that we aren't good enough and that the only way we are good enough is to buy more stuff.

This stripping of our self-esteem and self-worth (along with the injection of fear-based subconscious thoughts) is so insidious that it even gets you when you're on your game and cautiously watching out for it. For example, consider how when you travel a few days in a row, you can become a different person. Travel can be so competitive (upgrade, leg room, luggage space, small closed flights) that by the end of the week on the road, you've become an angry warrior. The airport competition and the general competitive nature of living itself shuffle you down this path toward aggression and sometimes anger. (Notice the theme of losing internal focus and allowing how attitude is molded by the external environment. You are surrendering to your surroundings). You have no real freedom and at times no dignity by the time you arrive at the weekend because you've spent time letting your environment rule you.

Is it any wonder that so few of us rise to any level of inner peace or greatness? Our external environment is loaded against us. It breaks up the conscious and subconscious alignment we need to hear the quiet, inner calling of peace, joy, happiness, and personal power. We are no longer free, but conditioned like robot satellites to stay in orbit around our selfish, fear-driven pursuits and ourselves.

Intentionality

When your conscious and subconscious minds misalign, you are going to have performance problems. You are going to experience distractibility, anxiety, fear, and anger within yourself and with others. You are going to live in a constant state of vague discomfort and become self-centered (inwardly focused) as you attempt to solve the discomfort you feel. This is a well trod and well understood feature of human thinking. Inner alignment is a crucial step in creating outer expressions of true greatness.

Properly aligning your conscious and subconscious mind and maintaining the alignment are what we call "intentionality." *Intentionality* is the mental convergence and focus: becoming consciously and subconsciously riveted on one purpose within yourself. It's about getting that internal focus and staying on it and repelling any external threat to your alignment. Intentionality allows you to take action toward anything with ease and relaxed certainty.

The path to true greatness includes the creation of a new subconscious core of intentionality, aimed at staying on a specific purpose, and making it operate smoothly and automatically. Greatness and true inner peace spring easily out of such a cognitive alignment. However, several things may be threatening to draw you away from conscious/subconscious intentionality:

- Brief attention spans and information overload
- Desperation that sets in with age
- Scarcity mentality

Brief Attention Span and Information Overload

Have you noticed that public messages of all kinds, especially commercials in the media, are getting shorter? This is because advertisers understand that information overload is epidemic in our lives. We only have a limited amount of conscious attention to invest (though it varies from person to person), and we all multitask to the best of our ability, but there are limits. How we allocate our limited brain resources is decided subconsciously, unless you make a determined effort to focus on or ignore something. But be warned: Mighty and determined forces are fighting for the attention of your mind, and your life is saturated with information designed to separate your conscious mind from your unconscious mind. Intentionality thieves are all around.

Desperation That Sets In with Age

Deep within us all lurks another dark force we must all manage. As we age, we become more and more aware of how we are doing in our lives. We ask ourselves all sorts of questions like:

- Is my life going as I planned?

- Why am I not as successful as my neighbor or that guy I went to college with?

- What is this all about?

- Am I living the life I wanted, or are am I just serving other masters, tramping out a living on a relentless treadmill?

These and other questions like them are universal in our culture. They begin when people begin feeling their mortality, which for both men and women is in their thirties through fifties. The emergence of these questions can bring with them a slew of new problems and issues. These difficult questions can begin to have a profound impact on your inner mental realm, and you can begin to feel out of alignment with yourself, as your subconscious yearnings clash with the realities of your conscious life. This clash can cloud your decisions and your activities and can often lead to deep restlessness.

The greatest people throughout history are those who have created a successful alignment between their conscious and subconscious minds. They've made peace with themselves; they've taken steps to decide what they want and don't want. Then they set about to create that reality in their moment-by-moment thinking and action. They've succeeded in creating inner alignment and in quieting the incessant questions that advancing age can create. We all must do this to attain what we call true greatness.

Scarcity Mentality

Nearly 30 years ago, Steven R. Covey wrote the classic *The 7 Habits of Highly Effective People*. In that book, Covey describes habits that define the classically powerful life. One of the habits he observed is the desire for highly effective people to create win-win outcomes. (Win-win outcomes are situations in which all parties in a dispute or disagreement are able to get what they want simultaneously. Everyone wins.) This is so vital that he went so far as to say if someone *doesn't* want to try to create win-win experiences in life, don't deal with them.

Win-win solutions need to be created because they don't often just present themselves plainly. They take effort and imagination. What destroys this creative effort is what Covey described as a "scarcity mentality." Though it has become a bit clichéd, the scarcity mentality is a brilliant description of a core subconscious issue that must be eliminated in order to achieve greatness. Covey explains what happens when people have a scarcity mentality:

> People with a scarcity mentality tend to see everything in terms of win-lose. There is only so much; and if someone else has it, that means there will be less for me.

Those with a scarcity mentality have a deep sense of hard limits and of scarcity. Subconsciously they think there are only so many deals to go around, only a certain amount of love you can get, only a certain degree of success anyone can attain, only a certain amount of money to be had, and so on. Their lives are governed at a subconscious level by a belief in hard, preset limits on literally everything.

Others have talked about this scarcity mentality too. Rosamund and Benjamin Zander, in their best-selling book *The Art of Possibility*, describe what they call the "calculating self" and the "central self." The calculating self coincides with Covey's scarcity mindset, in that it is totally consumed with survival in a world of scarcity. The calculating self is cunning, opportunistic, demanding, attention seeking, and selfish. As it turns out, scarcity and a fear of lack drives a lot of negative behaviors.

This is the root, or core, subconscious cause of a lot of conflict. Scarcity, as Covey describes it, causes extreme competitiveness, jealousy, an inability to share recognition, power, credit, or profit. You can't, for example, celebrate others' success because it means you didn't get it, and in fact it can even lead to your relishing another person's failures. Covey suggests an alternative mentality, what he calls an "abundance mentality."

> The more principle-centered we become, the more we develop an abundance mentality, the more we are genuinely happy for the successes, well-being, achievements, recognition, and good fortune of other people. We believe their success adds to . . . rather than detracts from . . . our lives.

Roz and Ben Zander refer to this as the "central self." The central self is creative, collaborative, giving, open, and kind. It is rooted in the expansive power of creativity and possibility to supply our needs, not the least bit concerned about superiority.

The abundance mentality is an acknowledgment that there is plenty to go around, that we get further ahead by cooperation, and that the world overflows with unlimited potential and possibility. It is like the old saying that a rising tide lifts all boats. This is a radical way to live, particularly when it bubbles from deep within your knowing, subconscious mind. Abundance thinking is an inner cornerstone of greatness.

The concept of abundance will enlarge and become more real to you as we move along over the next days and weeks. What is vital right now is for you to begin the action of seeing abundance around you and not allowing scarcity to seep into your expectations. Your emerging expectation of abundance in all areas of life serves as a good measure of how well you are expanding your internal mental framework.

How Do We Create a Fully Aligned Subconscious Intentionality?

Creating conscious and subconscious intentionality so that you are aligned and focused internally has been the goal of all personal change psychology for centuries. The alignment process pivots on how we actually learn things consciously and subconsciously and on how we then blend those learned lessons.

How we learn is a large area of study that continues to yield new and interesting information. For example, most of us believe that learning takes a great deal of time and effort. School taught us that we have to study hard to learn things. So we keep our noses to the proverbial grindstone, study, focus, rehearse, and re-peat over and over again until we get it.

This process works for learning many conscious things, but we can learn other ways too. We all have the ability to pick things up very quickly. For example, consider how you might learn about what happens to human skin when it's placed on a hot stove. If you take an academic approach, it would take a whole day of school to learn about formulas and equations for heat transfer, about how highly focused energy sources affect cell function, about autonomic nerve reactions, and about other esoteric concepts. Or you could touch a hot stove and learn all you need to know firsthand, so to speak. In a second, you take in a life-long, subconscious lesson. Our ability to learn certain things quickly and thoroughly is profound.

As already mentioned, advertisers and opinion makers use clever means to teach us at subconscious levels. They follow a very simple plan of clarity, simplicity, and repetition. First they craft a message that is clear, make it absurdly simple, and then put it in front of you over and over. That's it! It is a little less instantaneous than burning your hand, but it works well to influence you deeply for life. Just look around: You can control entire cultures of people if you are clear, simple, and repetitious.

So what does this mean for you? Well, you have to learn how to teach yourself lessons that stick in your subconscious. We are going to combine the focused conscious and the repetitious subconscious approaches to learning. Working with these two approaches, you can align greatness within yourself and make it start appearing in your conscious life, automatically springing from a new source deep within you. You will then begin having alignment, purpose, focus, and intentionality. These are the fundamentals of a life of true greatness.

What's Next?

It's time to see your world and its possibilities from a 180-degree shift: a *completely new perspective*. This view begins when you create a new inner process, a new way to organize your thinking and your efforts. Learning this information does not come by ramming it into your head like math tables. It's a distinctly different kind of learning curve. It is much like the difference between reading about burns and burning your hand: We want you to have an experience. We'll provide that experience to you in five steps. To help us explain this five-step unconscious core development process, we have created the Greatness Pyramid to help illustrate the progression from here to the place where you can run your own business and your life from a zone of subconscious greatness. It's the path to happiness and peace like you may have never experienced before.

CHAPTER 4

The Greatness Pyramid

※

Do not try to do great things
until you are ready to go about them in a great way.
If you undertake to deal with great matters
in a small way—that is, from a low viewpoint or
with incomplete consecration and wavering
faith and courage—you will fail.

WALLACE WATTLES

※

*This short chapter illustrates the steps for creating an
inner core of greatness. The whole system is built upon
five levels of experience, systematically stair-stepping to
the creation of a new subconscious core.*

A Very Brief Overview of What You Will Learn

There are five stair-stepping levels of exercises and tasks, each
designed to lead you to a more empowered knowledge of greatness. These steps are easy to take, and audio files are available on
line to further your efforts (www.beausay.com and www.drelko

.com). It won't be long before you will see new thinking and action appear in your life.

It may seem peculiar that changes could happen this way, but they do. Just think what fast food restaurant comes to mind when we say "I'm lovin' it!" or what car, beer, or soft drink you think of when you hear certain jingles or slogans. You've been thoroughly programmed by others without your knowledge or direct control to think certain thoughts when prompted. You've probably experienced the kind of learning we're describing tens of thousands of times in your life; you just didn't know it was happening. Now it's time to put that same process to work for intentionality and to take your life where you want it to go. You are going to learn to reprogram your subconscious-conscious mind alignment so that the thoughts you are thinking are the ones you have chosen to think. You are going to take over this process used by advertisers and others and learn how to do this to yourself.

The Greatness Pyramid

Get used to this image. It's vital for navigating the rest of this book.

The steps of this system are:

1. *Having a good picture:* Developing a clear image of who you are and what you want.

2. *Developing a clear process for doing what you do:* A stepwise,

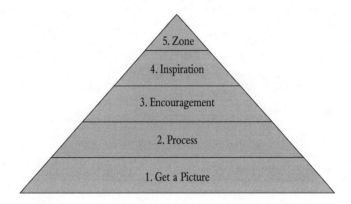

logical process you can refer to as you pursue true greatness.

3. *Learning the importance of encouragement (versus praise):* How to effectively get yourself back to your process and direct other people to theirs.

4. *The power of inspiring others:* Take outward steps to generate action in yourself and to create unusual impact on others.

5. *Getting in and staying in the selfless zone:* This is the place of your greatest power. As you apply the steps that have come before, a new life of focus, intentionality, and alignment emerges. True greatness and a sense of purpose flow from staying in this zone.

Several Things to Keep in Mind

Keep several things in mind as you go through this system. First, you will be cycling through this information several times. If an idea just isn't gelling in your mind, rather than grow frustrated, simply move on. Fitting these pieces together mentally takes different amounts of time for different people. If something isn't clear, keep reading and working and trust that everything will come together later.

Think through everything in the book and consider it non-judgmentally. If you know something only one way, then you really don't know it. So free your mind; this information is flexible and useful in a wide array of ways. Explore them and try things out. Your efforts to apply these ideas are critical.

Let's take a look at the first step: what it means to get a picture and get it pure.

CHAPTER 5

Level 1: Get a Picture and Get It Pure

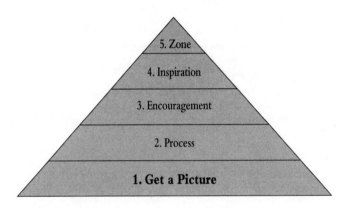

A fundamental principle of cognitive behavioral psychology is the proposition that inside all of us are two operating parts: you and something else commenting about you. "I said to myself" is a phrase we commonly use to describe our conversations with ourselves. The number one comment we hear from slumping athletes is, "I was thinking too much." In other words, I was talking to myself too much.

In the last chapter we discussed the importance of aligning the competing parts. This chapter discusses the importance of getting a clear picture of who you are and *what you want, discovering your "68" (your deepest, most profoundly passionate motive), determining what's real (that which is unchanging), and how to consistently feed this mental picture so that it surges into more power, focus, and purity as time proceeds.*

———

There are two mental attitudes a person may take.
One makes him like a football. It has resilience and
reacts strongly when force is applied to it,
but it originates nothing; it never acts of itself.
There is no power within it.
People of this type are controlled by
circumstances and environment.
Their destinies are decided
by things external to themselves.
The other attitude makes a person like a flowing spring.
Power comes out from the center of them.
They have within themselves a well of water
springing up into everlasting life.
They radiate force. They are self-active.
Wallace Wattles, *The Science of Being Great*

———

Life isn't about finding yourself.
Life is about creating yourself.
George Bernard Shaw, British playwright

———

Greatness Completes You

None of us likes to think of ourselves as selfish. Selfishness has bad connotations. It sounds small and unbecoming. Yet in reality, selfishness is something we all practice. It is just a part of the human psyche. We think ourselves at the center of the world, and consequently we want more and more. Wanting more is not a bad thing as long as your wanting is balanced. Of course, the lack of internal balance is a big contributing factor to major life dissatisfaction. How do you balance the natural urge for selfishness with a lifestyle of selflessness that brings true greatness? How do you live in such a way that greatness completes you?

Living selflessly requires some effort and retraining, and you may be thinking that there aren't many role models around to copy. That's not a problem, though, because you need to find your own style of true greatness. You are going to force yourself to be transformed by renewing your own mind on your own terms, not necessarily by directly observing others.

In his best-selling book *Winning*, former General Electric CEO Jack Welch says the secret to winning is to "change the way you think." The same goes with selflessness and greatness. Releasing true greatness is not accomplished through struggling to copy others, fighting hard all the time, practicing, studying, and learning as you might to build excellence. Instead, true greatness is built by a totally different approach: *undertaking to transform your thinking and allowing new behavior to flow effortlessly from it.*

When you want something you've never had, you have to

do some things you've never done. And that requires new thinking for the purpose of creating a lifestyle of selflessness and intentionality. Getting that new thinking activated is step 1: getting a
picture in your mind and getting it pure.

The Power of Vision

In the fall of 2001, the Miami Dolphins were playing the Oakland Raiders in an important interdivisional game. Jay Fiedler,
quarterback of the Dolphins, was having a terrific game when
late in the third quarter he was hit so hard he was knocked unconscious. When he finally came to, he was very woozy and had
to be helped to the sidelines.

He literally did not know who he was or what he was doing.
He could not even focus his eyes on his wrist band that contained
all the plays the team was using. Yet after several minutes he
regained his senses and began asking to be put back into the
game. Clearly dazed, he nevertheless begged the coaching staff to
let him play. They needed him, and soon he was put back into
the game, running the offense, now in the middle of the fourth
quarter and trailing the Raiders.

As the clock ran down, Fiedler pulled off one improbable
play after another, finally scoring the game-winning touchdown
with almost no time left in the game. His heroics were so notable
that he made the cover of *Sports Illustrated* that week. His daring
is still recounted with fondness in Miami.

When asked about how he made this dazzling comeback,

what Fiedler said was amazing. Jay had been the quarterback at Dartmouth University, an Ivy League school in New Hampshire, better known for turning out financial wizards than NFL quarterbacks. After graduation, Jay's roommate took a job as a trader with the gigantic New York investment firm of Cantor Fitzgerald in the World Trade Center. Because his job involved working the Far East markets, he worked on Tokyo time. When his shift ended on September 11, 2001, he left the north tower of the World Trade Center at 8:30 a.m. At 8:46 a.m., 14 minutes later, the first airplane struck the tower a mere eight floors below the offices of Cantor Fitzgerald. On that awful day, all 658 of the Cantor Fitzgerald employees who were in the office lost their lives.

Jay was nearly certain his friend was dead. Beside himself with panic, Jay called him on his cell phone, but he would not be able to reach him for days. When he finally did connect, Jay found him to be thoughtful and resolute about losing nearly all his friends. The lesson he passed along to Jay Fiedler was about vision, and his lesson was simple: "They will never terrorize me, Jay. I have made a decision that I will be the same person no matter what happens on the outside. I focus my vision on that every minute."

That was a lesson that was not lost on the young quarterback. And when he made his way back onto that field against the Oakland Raiders just months later, Jay Fiedler had incorporated that lesson into every facet of his game. He had a clear vision of what he was doing. He would compete with everything he had. The Oakland Raiders would never rattle him, and he would be the same person no matter how the game played out. Jay Fiedler told me that his clear vision made all the difference.

It's time for you to develop such a clear, empowering picture in your mind.

Where Are You Going?

Steven R. Covey became a guru by describing some very simple ideas about success in a compelling way. The first "habit" in his book *The 7 Habits of Highly Effective People* may have been one of the simplest: "Begin with the end in mind." It seems like a truism, but it's surprising how often this simple so-called aiming step gets overlooked in people's personal lives. So many people simply haven't the slightest idea where they are aiming themselves and their talent. And the truth is that you will never leave where you are until you decide where you want to be. As Mark Twain said,

> I can teach anybody how to get what they want out of life. The problem is that I can't find anybody who can tell me what they want.

Test this for yourself: Ask three people today where they are going in their lives. It's a simple question really, but the range of answers you get will probably be similar to the range you might get when you ask any personal question: a variety of laughs, hapless shrugs, resigned staring, worried glances, staring, or perhaps anger and impatient scowls at your nosiness.

These reactions are the norm. Rare is the person who can look you squarely in the eye and tell you plainly where they are going. Most people just haven't done the work of figuring it out. You can (and many people do) live an entire life with no plan or vision at all. In the pursuit of greatness, figuring out where you are going is your first job.

A case in point: I, Kevin, once spent four days at Disney World with my wife and kids. It was the last day of our trip, and I was wiped out. If you've been there, you know one of the popular attractions is a stage show based on the Disney movie *The Sword in the Stone*. We were exhausted, waterlogged, and sunburned, and I wasn't paying much attention. When the emcee asked for volunteers to come up and try to pull the sword out of the stone on the stage, I immediately sat back in my chair and made myself as small as possible. I wanted no part of any onstage performance. I just wanted to get out of that show and to get home.

While I was retreating from the emcee, another group of people were stepping up, anxious to be a part of the program. It was a group of young kids, all bald, wearing *Make-a-Wish of Tennessee* ball caps. As it turns out, these kids were there at Disney World as a last wish. The thought stopped me in my tracks. I sat in awe of these brave kids and their brave parents, enjoying, even for a brief moment, just a little fun before the greatest heartbreak in life would erase any happiness this park could possibly provide. I was humbled and embarrassed.

I learned a powerful lesson on that hot Disney day. Those parents and kids came to Disney World with a mental image to draw as much happiness as they possibly could out of that park. Their sole intention was to suck every drop of fun that place had to give. They were on a mission. And they succeeded, right before our eyes. I, on the other hand, had been, and, not surprisingly, I was miserable. We should all live with the positive intentionality of these kids.

The moral: A life driven by an *internal* intention of greatness has a better chance of success than one driven only by random *outside* forces. In other words, when you take action in the direction of greatness, your chances of success radically increase. As Wallace Wattles notes, it is a better attitude to be self-active and to radiate some kind of force than be a football.

What's the nature of that internal drive for you? How do you get one if you've lived your whole life being tossed by the whims of the world and never holding firm to a course that is your own?

The Conversation to Have with Yourself

The most basic concept of modern cognitive behavioral psychology can be summarized in a statement that we've all used:

I said to myself. . . .

Do you notice anything peculiar in this comment? What's unusual is that it implies the presence of two people inside your conscious mind: a speaker and a listener. This back-and-forth conversation between speaker and listener is a fundamental element of our thinking.

For years I, Kevin, worked with Bill Cowher of the Pittsburgh Steelers in the NFL combine, which is a gathering of college football players and NFL coaches that takes place in the winter. It is an important time to evaluate players (physically, mentally, and psychologically) and to make drafting decisions worth millions of dollars and the success of the entire franchise on the line. My job was to help evaluate players from a psychological perspective and to give my opinion of a player's ability to be coachable, productive teammates.

The first year we interviewed a moderately successful wideout from North Carolina State University. After he answered a series of football questions, I had my chance. I asked him simply if he'd ever faced any adversity. Yes, he replied, he'd separated his shoulder in college. Then I asked him if he ever played hurt. Yes, he replied, every single day of his college career he played hurt.

I put down my clipboard, a little shocked. *"Every day?"*

"Every day," he replied, "including games."

"How did you do that?" I wanted to know. His answer said more about him than a battery of psychological tests:

"Every day I went out onto the field *I said to myself,* 'If my mom can get up every day and go to work even though she had cancer, I can go to practice with a separated shoulder.'"

That player was a guy by the name of Tory Holt. Tory Holt went on to become a consistent All Pro receiver, Super Bowl

MVP, and world-class example of the power of talking to yourself, even taking yourself past deep physical pain.

This story illustrates the power present in conversations with yourself. It also clearly points out a direction of how you can begin influencing your own behavior. You need to take into account that a back-and-forth communication is going on in your conscious mind, and to a huge extent it controls the actions you take. Unlike the conflict between the conscious and the subconscious mind, this conversation can be heard and influenced directly and consciously.

Following a poor performance, the most common explanation athletes give for failure is, "I was thinking too much." That almost always means that a busy conversation going on inside their heads took their focus off what they were trying to do. *The conversation was a distraction from something that was vital to optimum performance.*

The internal conversation drew their minds off what they had seen themselves doing. The conversation caused them to lose the vision of what they were aiming for and began focusing on things that didn't matter (like the incessant inner chatter with your own mind). Poor performance always follows losing your purpose, losing your goal, and, in short, losing your vision. Staying focused on your vision is the fundamental first step for any successful endeavor, including the pursuit of greatness.

Getting Your Own Vision

Creating a vision for yourself has been talked about a lot. We've seen television commercials about it, and we hear the need for it repeated over and over in business settings, self-help workshops, life coaching, and other places. This isn't a new idea. The power of a personal vision has been known for thousands of years.

To the person who does not know where he wants to go
there is no favorable wind.

SENECA, ROMAN PHILOSOPHER

Where there is no vision the people perish.

PROVERBS 29: 18

The bravest are surely those who have the clearest vision
of what is before them, glory and danger alike, and yet
notwithstanding, go out to meet it.

THUCYDIDES (460–455 BCE)

Vision without action is a daydream;
action without vision is a nightmare.

ANCIENT JAPANESE PROVERB

Despite all this prompting, most people have no vision for themselves! Many of us just don't consciously choose a vision for ourselves, much less a great one. In most cases, the most fabulous and exciting visual guidance system we have available to us as functional human beings isn't even put into play. What happens instead is that, rather than choose any mental pictures, *we wait to have the pictures chosen for us.*

Think of sports. Visualizing success in sports is pretty easy because the goal is very clear: Either you score enough to win or you lose. In business and in life, winning is more subtle; keeping track of the score is not so easy, and it takes infinitely longer to play out the game. This all makes creating a picture that much more difficult and important. And the more subtle your task is, the clearer your visions must be. So whereas in sports it's enough to set your sights on, say, winning a national championship, in life you need to be more focused on coming up with a compelling goal and maintaining your aim for long stretches of time.

Most of us don't, or won't, do that. We allow our minds and our lives to drift, and either we don't take the time to develop a clear vision of where we are headed or we just don't know how. What almost all of us do as a replacement for creating our own internal pictures makes for the perfect storm of discontent: *We let others define the vision for us.* We let our bosses tell us what our goals are, we let our radio show commentators and politicians tell us what to think, we let our commercials tell us what consumables we desire, and so on. In the onslaught of all these forced visions, sometimes it's easier to just give up and be what you are told to be, even if it is not *who you are*, than to work to be *who you are.*

This is a very common experience. We get into a job and have certain goals, expectations, and corporate missions forced on us. We are asked to adopt those visions as our own and focus on them (as if we know how to focus in the first place). For many people, this externally injected picture suffices for them, and they're minimally successful. But for others who desire more from life than just contributing to corporate growth, anything less than your own well honed vision leaves you feeling unfulfilled and restless.

To break out of this corporate and cultural vision-injection process and begin manifesting your own greatness, you need to focus your own mind on your own vision. You need to refine *your* vision, the one that aligns properly and allows you to have intentionality. How do you get this special kind of internal vision? The fact is that your brain is a picture-making machine. You are making mental pictures right now. Pictures and images fly into and out of your mind constantly. The problem is that you aren't choosing them or controlling them. A projector is running in your head, all by itself, and you just watch.

There is a catch to letting the projector run on like this, and it's a little scary. Here's the rule: *What you consistently see in your mind you will consistently find.*

Several years ago, the Cleveland Browns had a quarterback by the name of Kelly Holcomb. He was looking forward to an upcoming game against their number one rival, the heavily favored Pittsburgh Steelers. It was certain to be a brutal game.

Going into the fourth quarter, Holcomb was having the statistical game of his life. In fact, by the time the game ended, he was just several yards short of 500 yards passing, a staggering yardage total that has been accomplished only a few times in the history of the game. He was the complete master that day, and, aside from a late game turnover that cost them the victory, Kelly's performance was simply magnificent.

After the game, Holcomb spoke about his outstanding play, and he said, "It came out *exactly the way I saw it*. I played the entire game in my head on Tuesday." Kelly proved what has become a certain fact: You get what you consistently see in your mind.

The questions you must ask yourself are, "Am I seeing what I want? Is it clear in my mind? Can I see with clarity what I am trying to accomplish?"

There is a somewhat famous story told of Walt Disney. It took place at the opening of Epcot center many years ago. Walt Disney had recently died, and his son Roy was escorting some dignitaries and newspaper reporters around the magnificent grounds. One of the newspapermen stopped Roy at one point and exclaimed, "It's too bad Walt couldn't be here to see all this." Roy turned to the newsman and said famously, "Walt did see it, that's why it's here."

If you think of the full implications of the power of your visualizing ability, it should make you break out into a cold sweat. The implications are these: If you think about good things, you will find good things, and if you think about bad things, you will find bad things. If you think about money, you will tend to find it. And if you think about poverty, you will tend to find it too. If you tend to think about random things, you will find random things.

I, Bill, often tell a story about a real estate convention at which I spoke. I was seated between two very pleasant, but very different women. They were both from Phoenix, the host city for the convention. The woman on the left won a sales award that evening. When asked about how the market was doing in the Phoenix area, she beamed, "It's great! I have more business than I can handle." The woman on the right was quiet throughout the dinner and awards ceremony. When describing the state of the local market, she glumly stated, "It's awful. Interest rates are bad, people expect the Taj Mahal when they should be in a double-wide, I can't get any cooperation from sellers. . . ." It won't surprise you that she won no medals that night.

It's like the story of the old farmer as he worked the field near his fence on the road one hot summer day. A tired stranger came straggling along, dusty and sweaty. He had a distant and unfriendly air about him, but he stopped long enough to ask the farmer what the people were like in the town up ahead. The farmer took off his hat, scratched his head, and asked the stranger what they were like in the town where he'd just been.

"Awful," he replied with a scowl. "Nobody talked to me, offered me any help or kindness in any way. I was so glad to leave."

The farmer looked at him and said, "Well, sir, I think you'll find the people in the next town to be the same way, I'm afraid."

A few hours later, another stranger came *whistling* down the road. His happiness was clear, and he cheerfully shouted a hello to the old farmer. "Say, friend," he said, "what are the people like in this town up ahead." The wise farmer sized him up and asked, "What were they like in the town you just came from?"

"Oh, they were the nicest people I've ever met. They all wanted to talk to me, I had several dinner invitations, and it seemed that nobody wanted me to leave."

The farmer smiled, took off his hat, and said, "I think you'll find the people in the next town to be exactly the same way."

The think → find formula is not 100 percent perfect, but it's perfect enough that we need to focus on it as a key to success on our journey to greatness. What do you visualize? What sorts of mental pictures are you making? How steady and reliable are they? Our visuals, if created haphazardly, can take us all over the place. For example, sometimes we visualize fun, happiness, and success, and yet at other times we see disaster, sadness, and poverty, depending on what life throws our way. We get a bill in the mail, visualize financial distress, and feel a cold chill and a pinch in the checkbook. Then we get a coupon for a free car wash and visualize how nice our car will look, feeling an instant burst of pride. Then we open a letter that says our kid is flunking out of school, and we visualize him or her going to jail. Then you get a call from a friend inviting you to dinner, and you visualize food and a pleasant evening.

It's no wonder our lives tend to be haphazard. Our internal visuals get pushed all around, created, and destroyed with the external ups and downs and swells of life. Most people just follow these haphazard visualizations. Sometimes they do that forever.

And by the way, it's no exaggeration that most people are better at visualizing disaster than they are visualizing success and happiness. Worry is so common. Just take a moment to think about the pictures that come into your mind when you're worried. Are they of happiness, success, confidence, and certainty? Probably not. The pictures we make in our minds when we are worried can actually make us feel worse. It's very common and very ordinary—not to mention practiced over and over.

Either we do this negative visualizing because we're living like corks bouncing on the tides of life or because we've never been taught a better way. There is a famous story told about the megasuccessful comedian and actor, Jim Carrey. Several years ago he was an obscure, $100-a-night stand-up comic. In an effort to bolster himself, he'd drive himself high atop the Hollywood Hills to sit in his car by himself and visualize. He says he would not let himself go home until he firmly believed in the pictures of success he was playing in his mind's eye. Only when he was euphoric from the success he pictured would he allow himself to go home. He says his return trip home was wonderful because he felt like all the wonderful things he had visualized were reality.

His devotion to visualization was so strong that one night he made out a check to himself for $10 million for acting services rendered. In 1990, when he was still a relative unknown, he had postdated the check for Thanksgiving 1995.

Here's what happened. He was paid a total of $800,000 for starring in *Ace Ventura, Pet Detective* and *The Mask*. As he says, it was good pay for him at the time—especially compared to earlier times when he'd drive 100 miles to perform for free. But the huge success of *Ace Ventura* and *The Mask* quickly catapulted him into a multimillion-dollar paycheck. He received $7 million for *Dumb and Dumber*. The really amazing part, however, is that just before Thanksgiving 1995, Jim Carrey signed a contract for $10 million.

"I wrote [the check] as an affirmation of everything I've learned," he told *Parade Magazine*. "It wasn't about money. I knew if I was making that much, I'd be working with the best people on the best material. That's always been my dream. If you give up your dream, what's left?"

We call that kind of mental focus "intentionality." Intentionality is seeing your picture, putting it front and center in your mind, and serving nothing but it all day long. Intentionality literally implies that you will find in your life what you are looking for and that you prepare yourself mentally to act with greatness before events even happen. Let's find out how to put intentionality into play and skillfully use the power of this visualization process to propel you to a different and better place.

Developing Your Authentic Vision

Creating a deepened and more focused vision for yourself, the one that accurately encapsulates who you are and where you will aim your selflessness, begins at a deceptively difficult place. To find that picture, ask yourself this: Beneath all the talk about careers, material possessions, social climbing, and all:

- What am I passionate about?
- What means the world to me?
- What can't I live without?
- What's unchanging about me, no matter how much success or money or fame I attain?
- Who am I?
- What do I stand for no matter what happens?
- What encapsulates what's deepest about me?

Dig deep into yourself. Take your time and do this well, even if it takes days or weeks. You may get many answers, and they may come to you quickly or slowly. Those who can answer these questions quickly and with certainty are rare. When you answer them yourself you'll be light years ahead of anyone else you know. It's the first step to creating a timeless, reliable mental vision for yourself.

What Life Was I Meant to Live?

Are you living a life that you thought was practical or what you accidentally wound up doing? Or are you spending every day working at the thing you love most? Most people find themselves doing jobs and living lives that they really didn't choose, but in some ways chose them. Consider one story of a successful and candid financial executive. She told us that in essence her goals were good, clear, and realistic for her job, but not really what she wanted deep down inside. Long ago, before she got into selling securities, she wanted to own a flower shop. She just loved the looks on the faces of those for whom she did flower arrangements—the beauty, the smells, the life. That was really what she wanted; it was her true dream.

Many people are just like this financial executive. Their lives are working fairly well, but they aren't doing what they really wanted to do. For some reasons, humans, like lemmings and sheep, are prone to following herd paths that have been established by those who have gone before them. Can you say that you are truly doing what you always wanted to do? Or are you doing what you were told you wanted to do? Of course, you can't just drop all your responsibilities to abruptly take a new path, but sometimes the disconnect between what you're doing and what you were meant to do is at the root of a lot of glaring life problems. And maybe, with some planning and forethought, a new path is exactly what you need to start out on.

Begin to probe yourself. Ask questions such as these:

- Away from my career, what sorts of questions interest me?

- What sorts of problems grab my attention?

- What sorts of dreams did I lay aside years ago but still percolate deep in my subconscious?

- What within me is dying to come out?

- What would be the most important things to do if I only had a year to live?

There is an infinite number of good questions to ask. For example, "Away from my career, what sorts of questions interest me?" You might come up with answers such as "How do computers work?" or "I wonder what it would be like to be professional rodeo clown?" or "Why isn't there peace in the world?" The range of questions and answers is infinite. What's important isn't having a right question but having a "you" question. What question is actually rising within you? Is it, "How can I become a more disciplined person?" or "How could I make the most of the days I have left?" or "Why am I so lazy?" Just make note of whatever questions arise from within you after you've thought a while. Just notice the questions and don't judge them.

There are two great days in your life: the day you are born and the day you know why. Think about that. You know the day your were born, but you need to ask questions that spear deep into your heart and subconscious to help you identify your why. Some people never figure out why, so consider yourself fortunate that you can begin making the inquiries into yourself to figure it out. Take some days, weeks, months—years, if you need to—and sort out the questions thoroughly. Your life success may ride on it.

What's Your Deepest Passion?

A huge and perhaps unexplored passion(s) exists somewhere deep in your mind. Subconsciously that passion(s) is your power source for living. Of course, you can generate passion for many things in your life, but the power of your deepest passions is unmatched. Forcing yourself to be passionate about something you're not truly and deeply passionate about often ends up being exhausting and, frankly, a whole lot of hard work. True greatness requires that you work the other way around; that is, you need to find the things that naturally excite your passions, then focus on them. This switch is not only energizing and effortless by comparison, but it is the path to consummate personal happiness.

It bears pointing out that businesspeople often focus on the technical skills and abilities of their jobs more than on their passion for what they do. They focus on giving perfect sales pitches or on understanding technical features of their product more than on finding positive benefits that excite them about their product or service. They are more concerned about making their sales numbers than by how much they love what they do. When passion gets replaced by technique, performance suffers and greatness slips away.

Focus on identifying your passions: What unlocks your deepest sense of urgency and power? Certain problems and challenges you face may do that. How about the things that tug at your heart? Inner emotional tugs suggest a deep and abiding passion hiding unseen inside you.

You may be loaded with these tugs and not notice them. Do this exercise, and you may find that you are passionate about many things. List two or three things that challenge you or grab your heart:

1. _____
2. _____
3. _____

These things have an unusual form of energy for you, and that energy will never go away. They suggest something about what is firm and unchanging in you.

You can find a similar list of passions if you think about the things that inflame your anger. You can learn a lot about yourself and your subconscious personality if you take note of the things that infuriate you. Strangely, anger can be closely associated with passions. If you can't find your passion, look at what makes you angry and follow the trail inward.

These suggestions will help you begin thinking outside the box about yourself and locating your hidden passions. They crack open doors you may have never known about and provide some basis for getting an empowered vision for your own personal greatness.

As a personal example of this, I, Bill, have been a full-time writer and speaker for years. I love writing and talking, but I have a strange and unexplained heart and passion for hungry kids. Ever since I first noticed that passion, I've actively contributed time to food banks, helped out at homeless shelters for families, and organized projects to help disadvantaged kids. Nothing fires my soul or leads to a deeper sense of purpose and meaning than doing these things. Though I love the profession of writing and speaking, helping these kids means true greatness to me more than writing, speaking, or nearly anything else. It's a passion that makes a difference for me and for others too.

> Man is so made that when something fires his soul,
> impossibilities vanish.
>
> JEAN DE LA FONTAINE

Another thought prompter to discover passions within has to do with understanding how life-changing events in your past have created great passions in your subconscious. One of the star players for the Pittsburgh Penguins a number of years ago was a young guy drafted from the Czech Republic (formerly Czechoslovakia) named Jaromir Jagr. Jaromir has since gone on to great things in the ranks of pro hockey. Throughout his career, he has insisted on wearing the number 68.

His reason teaches us a great lesson about passion and inner vision.

In 1968, Czechoslovakia was invaded by the Soviet Union, and many people were arrested and brutally persecuted. Jaromir's grandfather was arrested and died in prison. This experience burned a deep memory in Jaromir, and he committed himself never to forget his countrymen who had died bitterly and unnecessarily at the hands of the Soviets.

At the 1998 Olympics, the Russians were heavily favored to win the Olympic Gold in ice hockey. Jaromir had returned to play for the Czech Republic team, and they made it all the way to the finals against the mighty Russians. In his pregame locker room speech, Jaromir told the story of the rebellion, his grandfather, and what this big game against the Russians meant to him. He also revealed that this driving passion was what caused him to wear number 68.

His story was such a inspiration to the team that they beat the Russians that night and won Olympic Gold.

That number was a rallying point for Jaromir that summarizes all he is. That number is a potent reminder of what makes him tick. What event or events formed you? What makes you tick? What's your reminder? Write whatever picture, thought, word, idea, or internal mental movie that comes to mind.

_____

_____

_____

Sometimes the very thing in your core, your 68, is the most profoundly simple thing. South African Archbishop and Nobel Prize winner Desmond Tutu was once asked what prompted him to become a priest. He was quiet for a moment, then told of his

68. What he said in essence was, "When I was a very young boy, we lived in a place where black Africans were reviled. One day my mother and I were walking down a street, and a white man went by us and smiled and nodded with courtesy to my mother. That made a deep impact on me. That man was an archbishop."

Don't fret if you find discovering your 68 to be difficult. It may take some time to begin discovering or forming this sort of pointed, focused, and distilled mental picture. Some people take years to figure this out, and that's alright. What's important is seeing what is exactly right for you, knowing what causes your passions to stir, learning what is unchanging about your intelligence and what drives you at an emotional 68-type level. This is where your passions begin to reveal themselves. These passions come out of hiding and peek at you, if you are watching for them. There is a passion of some kind within you, and it's a driving power source you can learn to put into play. You put it into play by capturing it as a mental picture that you can see in your mind: *your 68*.

What Is Effortless for You?
What Makes Time Fly?

This is an easily overlooked area that frequently holds clues about your passion and intention. It is not uncommon to discount the value of what comes easily to us because something that comes easily seems to have less value. In fact, just the opposite is true. If something is effortless for you, if it is something that absorbs you and makes time fly for you, look at it carefully. It may be a hobby, a task, a job, a relationship, a routine—nearly anything. Whatever it is, it is a natural groove for you, a natural passion. Imagine doing that all the time? Even for a vocation!

For many, that thought sounds absurd. That groove is so natural and so easy that it appears to us to have no value whatever. But another way of looking at it is that not only does it have value but that *it's your value to give*. It's what you've been built to offer the world around you. It might be a talent such as an ability to tell stories or to decorate a house, a service such as offering your time to be a big brother or sister, a mindset such as optimism when things are tough for another person, a skill such as fixing cars, or an attitude such as being can-do when others are despondent or defeated. If it comes easily and totally absorbs your attention, it has value to the world in some way.

If You Had Just One Gift to Give the World . . .

You can discover much about yourself by asking yourself this question: "What's one thing I bring to the game of life? What's one thing that is my best gift? What is the one thing that will frustrate me the most if I can't share it with the world?" Don't judge any of this. For me, Kevin, it's simple. I have a mouth and I use it. For me, Bill, I have indefatigable optimism and can write. We use these gifts. They come as naturally to us as breathing. Shut them off and we'd suffocate. So we breath them in and out, and in doing so we find that our days are filled—*filled*—with energy, effortlessness, fun, and opportunity. And it's all because we found a way to give our unique gifts to the world.

Finding this gift may take some searching. The longer you've lived a life out of touch with your gifts, the more they may have melted into the background noise of your life. Don't let that slow you down. If you need to, ask some of your closest friends to give you some input. Think, keep a journal, and be wide open to your talents lying in places you least expect them. And don't be surprised if you discover you are the type of person who discounts a skill or gift out of embarrassment, judging what you have as of no real value to the world around you. Don't be like the lady most of us know who can sing like a bird, thinks of herself as a bad singer, and will never share her gift with a world that needs as much beautiful music as it can get. Always be alert to things that come naturally and easily to you, for therein you will almost always find your greatest gifts.

When I, Kevin, was addressing a group of 500 of the top financial advisors for a large investment firm, on the stage were the winners of the top producer awards for that year. After my keynote speech, an amazing man stood to tell this story. He said in essence that the keynote had opened up a new understanding for him. "I really wondered what my gift was," he said. "Then it hit me: My brother is a rabbi, and he saves spiritual lives. My sister is a doctor, and she saves physical lives. I'm a financial advisor, and I save financial lives."

Your special purpose in life may come to you at any time, even in a blinding flash. Be on alert for that.

What Do You Do with These Answers?

Your goal is to think about these questions so that you can create a mental picture that captures who you are in your deepest place. Your picture could be a movie, a mental image, or even a symbol if that works for you. The mental pictures people create are varied. Some people see themselves doing grand things like creating businesses that spin off huge cash for philanthropic purposes, creating world peace, or influencing global troubles. Others see more personal things for themselves, like being a better father or mother, giving time to the needy, or getting more active in a hobby. Still others see themselves doing extremely modest things like planting gardens, baking cookies for newcomers in the neighborhood, or being kind to bugs. All of these pictures are good if they come from the deepest part of you and reflect what you wish to give to the world around you. This is your elemental energy. You must find a way to tap it and put it into play in your life.

Other examples of these inner visions might be useful in guiding your search for your picture. I, Bill, have a vision of writing self-help novels that inspire action. I, Kevin, have a life-long vision of myself moving people to act in kindness. We've heard visions of people who want to create millionaires around the globe, wipe out AIDS in Africa, erase workplace backstabbing, create communication among people who live in great hostility, create paintings that brighten homes, participate in random acts of kindness groups, and so on. People who are successful in some realm of business have always been driven by the urge to give their time away to good causes like Big Brothers or the

Boys & Girls Clubs. A vision can be humble and personal, like feeding their family better, being kind to strangers, visiting sick people in hospitals, befriending people who live on the edges of society, and so on.

Everybody has his or her own unique picture to act on. Think about that carefully: *It's your picture!* One focused, solitary impression. Yours! Nobody else has it. Be proud of it because it is who you are. Find your picture, frame it in your mind, and make it pure.

How do you create a great, resilient picture and get it pure?

Your brain is pretty good at making pictures already: Just think of your passions, and pictures start popping up naturally. Once you have an image you're satisfied with, purify, clarify, and embellish it. Do all the things to it that you might do if your mental picture showed up on your television set all fuzzy and dark: Brighten the picture, give it great sharpness by focusing it, deepen the colors, expand the picture to be huge, like a movie screen, give it depth and brightness. You might have to take your time and close your eyes to do this well, but you'll find that with just a little bit of effort you can enhance any passion picture in countless ways. Make the picture of your passion a high-definition snapshot.

The reason for doing this is that our minds are very particular about how they handle pictures. That picture is the mental summation of your intention, and it must be clear at a subconscious level. Our brains think that the more real a picture *looks*, the more real it *is*. That's why we get so easily terrified when we imagine, for example, going bankrupt. We inadvertently create these images (big, full, brightly colored internal movies of destitution and loss) that terrify us because they seem so real. Our bodies think they are real and make you feel edgy and paranoid. Now you aren't thinking of these picture movies intentionally, but you are seeing some pretty scary stuff in your head. And remember that what you consistently see in your mind, you will consistently find, whether you're intentionally creating those mental pictures or not. To your brain, seeing is believing, so be careful what you allow it to watch.

In your conscious efforts to create your picture of greatness in your mind, take it a step further and make it twice as big, ten times as strong, and a hundred times more compelling. To see your internal pictures in this powerful way you may have to practice. Rehearsal works. Talk about it out loud if that helps. With practice you will get better and faster. Soon you will be able to create huge, bright, hi-def pictures in your mind on command. Get good at this: It's worth the effort.

What if You Don't Get Pictures in Your Head?

Some people literally don't make or see pictures in their minds. That's perfectly alright. If you are like this, you will experience your deepest passion converging into a thought, a phrase, or perhaps a statement or a sentence. You might even hear it or feel it. What matters is that you have some sturdy inner voice or phrase or representation that signifies your core intentionality. Allow your thinking to dictate what form your intention will take—visual, auditory, or feeling—and focus your attention on it.

What if Through Unseen Circumstances the Picture Suddenly Changes?

Sometimes, despite your sincerest effort at creating the right picture for yourself, everything changes. This can be as the result of a million possible circumstances. What's important to realize is that, no matter what changes in your life, your picture may have to adjust.

The Reverend Otis Moss of Chicago relates a powerful story of a picture that suddenly changed for a woman who was very dear to him. She was a parishioner, an elderly lady who suffered from an advanced stage of diabetes. She was told she would have to have one leg partially amputated. This was devastating news to her because she was very active and moved around a lot.

When he visited her in the hospital post op, he learned that the circumstances had changed. The doctors discovered that the damage from her diabetes was more widespread than they thought, and they needed to amputate both legs. She was completely devastated, but her response is the model for handling situations where circumstances change your vision.

"My mother once taught me how to crochet and knit," she told Reverend Moss. "I think I'm going to start doing that. And she also taught me how to bake pies. I haven't baked pies in years. Do you like pies, Reverend Moss?" she asked.

"Yes I do," he replied.

"Then I'm going to make you the best pie you ever tasted."

When your life circumstances change, bake a pie.

What's Next?

Eventually we will have to entertain the question: *Is there enough evidence in your life to convict you of your picture?* But don't worry about that now. At this point, it is important just to have a picture, a phrase, or an inner knowledge of what accurately represents your deepest inner passions. The ability for greatness resides in all of us, and your passion is the trail that will lead you there.

With a clear picture in mind, you know what you're aiming at. For now, don't worry about how you're going to make that picture happen. Thinking about the how of making the pictures reality just distracts us from the search for the what. When the what is clear and focused, the how will mysteriously emerge, often in the most unlikely ways. Let's create a process, cycle through it, and bring your picture into greater clarity, power, and reality.

—⊸∞⊸—

Can you think of anything more permanently elating than
to know that you are on the right road at last?

VERNON HOWARD

—⊸∞⊸—

CHAPTER 6

Level 2:
Create a Process

This chapter discusses a step-by-step process for strengthening your picture and making it a constant part of your behavior. We go into detail about honing this process until it's streamlined and smooth and about connecting all the errant dots of your life into one dynamic, focused force. A strong picture (step 1), supported by a strong process (step 2), can increase performance manifold, blending business success and interpersonal energy into one force.

———⊗⊗⊗———

You gotta create a dream. You gotta uphold the dream.
If you can't, go back to the factory, go back to the desk . . . .
ERIC BURDEN

———⊗⊗⊗———

What Do We Have Now, and Where Do We Go Next?

Your picture, your core, or the intention you uncovered in the last chapter is, in a sense, more "you" than the outward face you show the world. It drives and energizes the deepest parts of you. How can you translate that vast part of you into action and be responsible to usher it into fuller expression in your life? That is the role of your process.

Few people have a picture; fewer still have a process. When you make creating and using this process a healthy obsession, your picture becomes the self-regenerating power source you need it to be. Of this healthy obsession Alexander Graham Bell said,

> What this power is I cannot say. All I know is that it exists. And it becomes available only when you are in the state of mind which you know exactly what you want, and are fully deter-mined not to quit until you get it.

The last chapter was about *exploring* options for what your picture should be. It was about searching through your experiences to define what makes you tick. Creating a process *eliminates* options. The step-by-step process you create in this chapter is the bridge from your inner picture to your outer behavior.

You need a process because your drive toward true greatness will be tested.

Chuck Noll, the legendary Hall of Fame coach of the Pittsburgh Steelers, said, "Pressure is what you feel when you don't know what you're doing." In almost every case we know of, when people have a problem with a diet, money, a career pursuit, parenting, or anything in life, the reason almost always boils down to a lack of a process that tells them what to do. They may understand their goal, but they don't understand themselves and how their haphazard inner organization keeps them from achieving their goal. They have no process to rely on for guidance.

People who reach great success always have a process: a concrete, step-by-step system that is simple and repeatable. Most successful people can describe what they did and what pattern they followed to achieve their successes. This is true in sports, business, education, and nearly any other pursuit. The normal conduct of life challenges your focus. You need a system of keeping your eye on the ball. Chances are good you will never hear about those who had no plan or system like this because they will fall victim to distractions. The secret of true greatness is hidden in the routine or process you create.

What Is a Process?

A process is a concrete series of thoughts, words, images, prayer, or dialogue you use to mentally and physically drive *yourself back to your core picture.* A process does not create greatness in itself but rather serves as a reliable step-by-step series of actions that puts you back into your picture.

This series of actions can be as extensive as paragraphs of words or written-out steps or as simple as a single visual representation or icon. In business, McDonald's has a simple and reliable method of making hamburgers. The process does not change from store to store. The process is tried and true and turns out perfect McDonald's hamburgers every time. Supercut's Hair Salons have four kinds of haircuts: 1, 2, 3, and 4. Each of those cuts is a process that doesn't change from one store to the next. It's a reliable and concrete series of simple steps that leads to a result. The well-known feel-felt-found process is used by master persuaders to get people's attention and cooperation: "You feel ripped off. I've felt ripped off before too, but I found. . . ." Tom Myslinski is a strength/position coach for the Cleveland Browns. Tom is methodical in how he thinks and coaches. He also has an intuitive understanding of process. He never tells his players just to "go and knock people down." Rather, he harps constantly on the fundamentals of blocking: "Set your weight properly, keep your hands high and your head back . . . ." Chad Lewis, star NFL receiver, doesn't just "go out and catch the ball." His process, perfected with endless repetition, is, "Release from the line, look for the ball, find the 'X' [the stitching on a football looks like an X as it's traveling toward you], catch the ball, tuck it, run." He practices that process over and over and over in his thoughts and actions. These guys know exactly what they want, and they have a simple process for getting it.

You may be asking yourself, why not "just catch the ball"? Or why not "just be successful"? Why not "just be great"? Your process allows you to remain focused on *what catches the ball*. Your process allows you to remain focused on *what creates success*—and greatness. It relieves the stress and tension that can destroy performance and allows you to focus on the step-by-step of accomplishing something from a new mindset. In short, it frees you from the very pressure that destroys most people's best efforts.

To remain focused on who you are and what you wish to accomplish professionally, create a list of three or four steps you can practice. The list will change as you read it over and consider how it's working for you. You will mentally rehearse these steps throughout your day. Your three- or four-step process will keep you rooted in your picture.

A Process Will Always Do Four Things

To confront and overcome the challenges to your process, make sure your process focuses you:

1. On taking responsibility.
2. On controlling what you can control.

3. On staying on purpose.

4. Away from acting on feelings.

1. Taking total responsibility

A process helps you take total responsibility for what's happening around you. Nothing great happens until you take total responsibility for what's going on. Don't ever blame others for failures that may have contributed to your failure to reach your own true greatness. You must adopt an attitude of total responsibility for your participation in the ongoing conduct of your life.

The truth is that sometimes other people's faults or faceless circumstances line up against you, but don't dwell on them. Don't play the blame game or point fingers. Absorb all the responsibility for yourself. Why? Because when the responsibility is in your hands, you can do something to change things. Don't ever give up the power to take action by avoiding or shirking responsibility. Assuming responsibility is the ultimate way to disarm anger and to regain power. No self-pity: It's the law.

2. Control what you can control

A process helps you control the only thing you can really control. During the Vietnam War, A. J. Muste, an internationally renowned pacifist, was seen every day for a year, standing in front of the White House with a candle in his hand. Rain or shine,

A. J. stood as a sentinel, quietly calling attention to the insanity of the Vietnam conflict.

One day a reporter approached him with some questions. In short, the reporter wanted to know what he was doing and why he was doing it. After a brief explanation, the jaded journalist got right to the point. He looked at Muste and said, "You know this isn't going to do anything. You aren't going to change the world by standing here with a candle." Muste looked thoughtfully at the man, then replied quietly, "I am not trying to change the world. *I'm making sure the world doesn't change me.*"

The world around us is largely beyond our control. The only thing you can reliably control is yourself. You can't stop the world from going about its madness, but you can guard yourself and control your thoughts, attitudes, responses to challenges, and other actions. At some level in your mind, you must make a decision that you will constantly stand on your own, independent of others, and on your own terms. In essence you declare to yourself, "This is who I am, this is who I am going to be, and I'm not going to join with other people or be who they expect me to be. And I will never expect less of myself because everyone else is making that choice."

The great writer Anna Quindlen said,

> The thing that is really hard and really amazing is giving up being perfect and beginning the work of becoming yourself.

Becoming yourself and living as yourself are among the most noble and powerful things any person can do. You get to that place not by trying to control the world, but by devoting energy to focusing on and becoming the master of yourself.

3. Stay on purpose

A process reminds you of your purpose. Being on purpose is no more complicated than reminding yourself often of what your vision is really all about. Being and staying on purpose may take a while to ingrain and to become automatic, but take time out daily—many times daily, if need be—to remind yourself of your purpose.

Some people find it helpful to write down these pictures, intentions, and life purposes. We both, Kevin and Bill, keep journals of thoughts, ideas, and memory prompts to help us remember what we want to focus on about ourselves. When the bullets of life start flying, it's very easy to lose track of what you are trying to accomplish, of your mission, and of your vision. The end of your enthusiasm and zest for living comes soon after that.

To stay on purpose, you must find a way to feed your internal vision. You must avoid allowing your picture to drift into mere mental entertainment. That is called daydreaming and means certain death to your intentionality. The difference between focusing on vision and daydreaming is intention. Are you intending on bringing your inner vision to life within your mind, or are you simply allowing your mind to wander aimlessly through images and ideas? Only you can know for sure. What you want, when you use your process and see your picture, is an inner surge toward power and focus and action. A process takes you to that place of strength with regularity and power.

4. Don't operate from feelings

A process helps you to operate your life from a plan, not as a simple reaction to your ongoing feelings. Tony Dungy, head coach of the Indianapolis Colts, is one of the kindest, most respected, and loved coaches in all of football. But despite the warm, feel-good vibe of this guy, his process appears to be to love his players, to encourage, and to correct them—but team first. One time he was in a practice with a player who would become one of his favorites, Hardy Nickerson. Hardy was a real gamer: high-strung, intense, and prone to overdoing it on the practice field. Dungy warned him several times to quit hitting people after he blew his whistle. And though he loved Hardy's aggressiveness, loved his talent, and loved his passion, Dungy had a process that he wasn't going to change.

After blowing his whistle many times and watching as Hardy failed to stop his intense play, Dungy had had enough. He felt like screaming. But rather than blow his top, he asked Hardy to leave the field and forbade him to play that week. Did he feel like doing this? Of course not. His feelings and admiration for this guy were enormous, but he had a process he was not willing to abandon for a good feeling. By choice, his commitment to his process was stronger than his feeling.

A similar story is told about an El Salvadoran doctor known

only as Dr. Juan. He was a physician committed to his passion of helping anyone in need, anywhere and at any time. His process was simple: If you find people in need, no matter who they are, you treat them, for they are human and worthwhile. For his efforts he was censured by the El Salvadoran government for helping people it considered to be threats. His primary tormenter was a man by the name of Colonel Arturro, who was bent on destroying this pest. But Dr. Juan was true to his process. He continued to help people no matter who they were. For that Arturro would have Dr. Juan beaten and stabbed, his wrists slashed, and finally shot and left for dead.

Were it not for the help of some close friends, he would have died. His gunshot wounds were so serious that through the help of sympathizers in the government, he was smuggled out of the country and ended up in New York City, where he received lifesaving surgery and in time was able to set up a small medical practice for El Salvadoran immigrants.

Some years later, after a regime change in El Salvador, Dr. Juan was working in his New York City clinic. To his utter disbelief, a man he recognized from El Salvador entered his office. It was Colonel Arturro, in bad need of help. What might you have done? Dr. Juan had committed himself to a process, and feelings, inflamed as they might be, would not interfere. Though he recognized the cruel military man, his process was ironclad, and he offered him medical assistance. The two men became good friends, proving that commitment to a process can bear fruit in the pursuit of true greatness.

Create Your Process

Begin by creating a three-step process. For example,

- Step 1: Sit quietly for five minutes and review your picture in your mind.

- Step 2: As you view your mental picture, write in a journal any new pictures or thoughts that pop into your head that inspire you.

- Step 3: Immediately find a way to put a piece of your picture into play today.

Be as creative and detailed as you like, but keep it simple. There is no particular need to invent a process that is overly complex; you are better served by keeping it simple. Make it boring if need be. *Just remember that the purpose of this process is to quickly and effectively take you back into the high-definition picture of who you are in your deepest place.*

Tom Brady of the New England Patriots is widely regarded as one of the most successful quarterbacks ever to play professional football. What's most interesting about him, however, is the fact that he's not the biggest, certainly not the fastest, not the strongest, or, frankly, not the most gifted athlete in the league. What sets him apart is his consistency: Nobody in the league is better at methodically and accurately reading defenses, play-calling at the line, running through progressions of receivers, and so on.

You could easily say he is the most boring quarterback in the league.

Be boringly consistent on your process, even if you find yourself adjusting it. The truth is that sometimes your process can become stale or unworkable and needs to be refined or adjusted. That's fine. Hone it and change it as needed. Just be sure that your process continues to focus you:

- On taking responsibility.
- On controlling what you can control.
- On staying on purpose.
- Away from acting on feelings.

Do your steps with such repetition that they become instinctive for you. Nothing will bring you repetitive success like a process.

Here's an example of how my (Bill's) process works. My deepest passion is to spur people to achieve their own unseen potential. My picture is of people coming into my presence and feeling challenged, hopeful, and empowered. My process is to:

1. Pray for focus.

2. Reaffirm my vision by taking a few seconds to immerse myself in it.

3. Take one step toward action—any action.

4. If the desired result is not emerging, get away from people and take a longer time to refocus.

5. Share my gratitude for my life and vision with someone else.

6. Call in support from my team; they've been trained in what to do.

I run through this sequence like Tom Brady checks off receivers, and taking as few as one to three of these steps gets me right back into my picture, empowering and equipping everyone I come into contact with. Take note that these steps by definition keep me responsible, keep me controlling the only thing I can control (me), keep me on my purpose, and focus me away from my feelings.

Your Commitment to Greatness Will Be Tested

Expect your commitment to greatness to be tested, starting right now. That's why you need a process. As soon as you begin taking steps in the direction of greatness (such as creating a vision as you did in the last chapter), an entirely new flock of challenges will rise to intercept you. Your challenges will come from two sources:

1. External sources like people, events, and circumstance

2. Internal sources like your own learned habits and practiced tendencies

The weakness of many personal change approaches is that they fail to teach you specifically what to do when you slip up or collapse. The truth is that you will slip up along the way, but stumbling doesn't mean you will fail. Instead, you will have to be prepared for setbacks. Resilience in the face of challenge or breakdown doesn't just happen by accident. It is planned, and it must be learned like anything else. Before we go into how to build a process, let's examine the probable challenges and distractions.

You are likely to face four specific challenges:

1. The unconnected dots of your life

2. The tyranny of the moment

3. Critics

4. The gambler's fallacy

1. Connecting your dots

Remember the childhood game of connecting dots on a sheet of paper to reveal a picture. It was pretty high entertainment for a first grader, at least in pre-Internet days. But it is actually a great metaphor for describing all that you carry about in your head.

Our minds are a complex tapestry of thoughts, ideas, emotions, dreams, and other things. Some of those pieces are connected together, others are free floating and not connected to much of anything. Combine all the disparate pieces, and that combination becomes you.

But we all are naturally driven to make sense of ourselves. We are curious and sometimes troubled about the parts that don't fit well with the other parts. For example, we might feel very driven to accomplish great things with our career, yet feel generally lazy and unfocused. These two inner pieces war with each other and cause varying degrees of frustration. People say, "I can't figure myself out" . . . "What's the matter with me?" . . . "I just can't get it in gear" . . . and so on. You've probably done that in one or many areas of your life. Usually, we keep those warring parts hidden, but functional people attempt to make them fit together.

Those parts are simply experiences. We have literally millions of them. We refer to these experiences as your dots. Getting your dots (experiences) connected and having them make sense is, for most of us, a lifelong pursuit. Most people are unable to do that in an organized way, but you can.

Without connecting the dots in a meaningful way, you will continue to labor with the challenge and distraction of unconnected pieces of your own experience that don't fit. Conversely, when your picture is clear, your intentionality will have no competition and you'll easily zero in on what you need to do. Other pictures may come into your head but they can't compete with the clarified, focused one—the one that is the real you.

I, Kevin, shall never forget standing on the sidelines as my beloved Steelers played the Dallas Cowboys several years ago. I'd been a psychological consultant to many pro and college football teams by this time and had just spent some time helping do my part to prepare the Steelers for this big game.

The Cowboys had held us on a third-down play and we had to punt on fourth down. Onto the field came one of the most feared punt returners in the history of the NFL: Dallas Cowboys star Deion Sanders. As he came onto the field during a television time-out, he was yelling at our bench.

"Which side of the field do you want me to return this?" he taunted.

The Steelers, never to be outdone, screamed back, "This way, Deion! Come over here. We're gonna kill you!" Pro football players are clear communicators.

We kicked the ball, a great punt, and it drove Deion deep toward his end zone. He had plenty of room to field the kick and immediately turned toward our sideline and came toward us. He juked a few of our guys and cut up the sideline, passing right by us, smiling and waving. He ran for an outrageously in-your-face touchdown. The Cowboys beat the Steelers that day and he hasn't forgotten it.

The next year, I started working with Dallas and got to know Deion. I discovered that, for all his public escapades, he was a man who wanted desperately to connect the dots in his life, and learn to handle the enormous pressure that surrounded him constantly.

On the first day of camp, I saw an example that changed my view of both Deion and dots. To my surprise a bunch of Cowboy fans were sitting up in the stands, taunting Deion.

"We hate you, Deion!" . . . "Deion, you suck!" . . . "Get out of town, Deion!"

Sanders had a polarizing effect on people that way.

Now, *what would you have done in that situation*? It's a difficult question that can be handled many ways, depending on how your dots are connected. Write down your reply before you go any further:

_____

_____

_____

Here's what Deion did: He coolly pointed at one of his hecklers and asked him to come down to the fence separating the players from the fans. As the fan approached, Deion leaned into the fence and asked him to come closer. What he then did was unforgettable and reflects the kind of personal power available to someone who is willing to privately connect his experiences in intentional ways.

He pointed at the man and said, "God bless you."

The astonished look on the face of that fan suggested something unique had just occurred. It was a snapshot moment that drove home a lesson for me; when someone decides to connect the inner dots to make a difference, then practices and prepares, magic can happen.

Did Deion's reply have the ring of greatness? Yes, it did. We judge it as true greatness because it came from an inner core of connected dots. It didn't happen just by accident: Deion mentally prepared for that moment before he even set foot on the field.

He was clear on the picture of the persona he wished to project. He had to have mentally prepared for the moment because his reply was just that rare and jolting. His mind was aligned for it and he'd decided to act that way. His reply was generated from an entirely different way of thinking than most ordinary human emotional reactions. It was almost otherworldly. He was clearly using a different, more profound way to think and act than is common. He was not stretching, straining, or reaching for greatness either; you can't stretch for something so awesome. That demonstration of inner togetherness came from time spent connecting inner dots.

Connecting all your dots will be a lifelong effort. Our brains just get cluttered with memories, insights, corrections, and the like, and the pieces need to be culled, connected, or cleaned out. It's what makes us human. As you move through the latter portions of this book, we will delve more into dealing with this mental clutter.

2. The busyness of life can pull us off our process

In his best-selling book, *The Tyranny of the Moment*, Thomas Hylland Eriksen describes our 21st-century lives as cramped and fully occupied by things that don't really matter. "All our technology has led to higher and higher stacks of information that lead nowhere. Technology has become our best friend and our worst enemy."

He goes on to talk of what he calls "slow time" (quiet, reflective moments) as our most valuable resource, one we must fight to preserve. "As availability [of free time] approaches one hundred per cent, the struggle now concerns the right to be unavailable, the right to live and think more slowly."

Our lives are jammed with duties and responsibilities. We have an almost knee-jerk, jump-to-it reaction to the phone ringing, we get hives if we can't check our email, and God forbid your Internet connection goes dead. We've created a monster in our technology, and we now serve it sometimes to the detriment of our own lives, passions, and well-being.

We've handed over personal control in other areas of our lives, including extracurricular events, family duties, second jobs, school, clubs, and other arenas. The reality is that there is often little time to really hone in on your passion, and your process gets lost in the din of everyday life. We just get too tired, too distracted, and too preoccupied with the demands of daily life.

Becoming a person of true greatness requires you to control your schedule, not allowing your schedule to control you. Simple time control may be your biggest challenge. As an experiment, sometime in the middle of the busyness of a normal day, try to stay intentional on your passion, your image of greatness, your message, or the picture you've created. Do it just for a few minutes and observe what happens. You will feel the powerful demand of your day-in, day-out life calling for your immediate attention.

That is your challenge. That is what your process is created to help you contend with. It should work to give you a step-by-step process for staying focused on who you want to be. *If it fails to do this, start over and simplify the steps until you create a process that works in real life.* This is your challenge.

3. Critics

You should expect that, if you seek to turn your picture into a reality that is an advancement over who you used to be, some people will ridicule you. There are people out there who are just not going to be happy with your being focused and successful. It's just human nature—pure jealousy on the part of others. If you want to be great, you have to be willing to stand alone and deal with critics.

Frequently, tension builds between those going forward and those treading water. Some may think that "If I can't do it, neither will you." But the rewards for going forward despite the unspoken jealousy of naysayers far outweigh the risks.

———

You are not made great by the location in which you happen to be nor by the things with which you may surround your self. You are not made great by what you receive from others, and you can never manifest greatness so long as you depend on others. *You will manifest greatness only when you begin to stand alone."*

WALLACE WATTLES

———

As you will experience in the next chapter, getting your process in place plays a huge role in handling critics. Once your passion and picture are clear and pure and once you have a process to keep you on the picture, the criticism of others has far less impact on your mind.

4. The gambler's fallacy

The gambler's fallacy is an interesting and instructive piece of the human behavior puzzle. In general, the gambler's fallacy says that if you win a bet, you will continue to bet the same way and that if you lose a bet, you'll change your bet. You can easily test this fallacy for yourself. Take a coin, flip it, and call it in the air. Then repeat the process. Then repeat it again. Keep track of which you call heads and which you call tails.

Most people think about changing their call following each flip. If you changed your call, on what did you base the change? Was your new call based on a system of some sort or on your gut feeling? Do you base your call on how the coin landed previously? Most people have simple mental explanations for how they guessed heads or tails, and none of the explanations has anything to do with reality.

In reality, each flip has a 50/50 chance of landing as you called it, no matter how many times you've flipped. There is no measurable force acting on it other than random chance to make a series of five heads go heads again. What changes is you and your thinking about how you should act based on different variables.

The gambler's fallacy is responsible for a lot of people losing lots of money and losing precious time in their lives. Here's why: If something works, we have tendency to repeat what we just did. If it fails, we have a tendency to change our bet because the experience of losing is more powerful than that of winning. We also have a tendency to become superstitious about what is and isn't working. Gambler's-fallacy thinking plays a huge role in how you run your own life. If something in your life is working (whether it's good or bad for you), you will tend to repeat it. And if something fails to work, you will change your behavior quickly. Rare is the person who will stay with a bet when it appears not to be working.

Can you see how this relates to your behavior with your process? If your process works, you will continue it. But if it fails, your human tendency is to change the bet and do something different. It is vital that you stay with your process whether or not it appears to be working. Don't let the failure of your process to work dim your attempts at staying with it consistently. Many people have abandoned their dreams and passions in the mistaken belief that they were on the wrong path—doing the wrong thing—when in fact it was just the gambler's fallacy playing games with their resolve.

In developing and following a process, you must prepare yourself to ignore your instinct and feelings and refuse to be controlled by this fallacy. How do you do that? Decide on your bet (your process), and stay with it no matter what happens. The odds are that your process will deliver with consistency.

Now It's Your Turn

On the following lines, write out three steps to get you back to your picture. Just make a start. This list will evolve as you practice and find what works just for you.

1. _____
2. _____
3. _____

Just make sure these steps make you responsible, allow you to control what you can control, keep you on purpose, and prevent you from relying on feelings.

Sometimes, when creating a personal process, you might go blank and not know what to do next. That means you have no process for thinking about a process, and you might feel stuck and unable to create any meaningful steps to follow. You can remedy that by intensifying different attributes of your mental picture. Make your inner picture, which is visual, more compelling by amplifying the other four accompanying senses: hearing, feeling, smelling, and tasting. For example, as you envision yourself providing shoes for impoverished tribes in Mongolia, bring the picture to life by making the other nonvisual senses more intense: Add your voice and other voices to the picture, touch the shoes, feel what the environment is like, smell and taste it if you can. Immerse yourself in your mental image by including all the senses. This simple exercise intensifies your inner experience, making it more real and compelling.

The more senses you bring in to this picture this way, the more real your inner focus becomes. And the more real it becomes, the higher the probability is that you will create a process pathway to keep it happening in your life.

Getting careless or lazy and failing to successfully embellish your inner experience renders your inner image boring and uninteresting. Don't shortchange yourself: Fill in the picture with power and depth. Make it compelling and real in any way you can.

Embellish your picture for 20 or 30 seconds three times a day, in addition to running your process. Immerse yourself in that inner experience. The picture will grow to new levels of intensity as you add these dimensions of sensory experience. Make the quest a daily requirement and develop the habit of simply immersing yourself in the ever intensifying image. It is, after all, what your process is aimed toward reminding you of. And the more effective you become at eliciting that inner picture, the closer you come to realizing outer greatness.

What's Next?

In this chapter, you explored the path to creating a simple one-two-three process to get you back to your picture when you drift. Take your time to create a step-by-step system of some type. Create it, test and retest it, and re-create it if need be. Work your process until it works to reliably point you back to your unshakable core. Do not settle for a process that doesn't get the job done. In the next chapter you are going to examine another way to keep you on your process and how to use encouragement to point you in the correct direction.

CHAPTER 7

Level 3: Encouragement

In the last chapter you created a simple step-by-step process that takes you back to your picture. Your next level in the five-tier system is encouragement, and this is a big deal. Encouragement can be directed toward one of two ends: an outcome or a process. For example, when it is directed toward an outcome, you focus your effort at achieving a win or a score. The more uncommon and more powerful form of encouragement, however, focuses your effort back to your process rather than at a specific objective like a win or a score. A more powerful way of encouragement is to say, "I will stay focused on making the sales calls I need to make every day successful."

Such encouragement takes you right back into your process.

———❧———

What we need is not to be taught new truths,
But to be reminded of the truths we already know.
SAMUEL JOHNSON

———❧———

The most common form of human stupidity
is forgetting what you are trying to do.
FRIEDRICH NIETZSCHE

———❧———

Reaching Out

Billy Martin was hired and fired as manager of the New York Yankees six times. After one of those firings, Yogi Berra was hired to manage the team. When he arrived in his office on the first day, he found two envelopes from Billy Martin. One said, "Open in an Emergency" and the second one said, "Only Open in an EXTREME Emergency."

The Yankees promptly went on a six-game losing streak, and the media, the fans, and management were coming down on Yogi. In desperation he opened the first letter. Inside the letter was a note that said simply, "Blame everything on me." Yogi Berra did just that and it worked: The media and fans backed off, and the management calmed down. Indeed, the team began playing better.

Then the Yankees went into a deeper slump, this culminating in a nine-game losing streak. Once again the media and fans were going crazy, and management was getting hot as well. Yogi Berra went into his office, closed the door, and opened the second envelope titled "Only Open in an EXTREME Emergency." The note on the inside said, "Prepare two envelopes . . . ."

Though we can't verify that this humorous anecdote is true, it illuminates our need for encouragement. We all face significant uphill challenges in our lives, and an encouraging word can provide relief and direction to others. Though the encouragement offered by Billy Martin in this story is not exactly what we're talking about, learning to encourage effectively can have powerful results not only in others, but in ourselves.

Encouragement, as it is commonly used, aims at "giving courage" to someone in pursuit of a specific outcome. It's the old rah-rah stuff we've all used and heard: "Take that hill!" . . . "C'mon, you can close that deal" . . . "You're smart enough to get an A." . . . "Win one for the Gipper." And so on. There are upsides to this kind of interpersonal bolstering, but some downsides too.

The upside is clear. People's courage and belief in themselves falter from time to time, and hearing good words from someone else can be the difference in giving them renewed energy and hope. That renewal of hope and the injection of energy have the power to get people believing again and taking action. Strong words of encouragement can affect another person's belief system and provide a needed shot in the arm to resuscitate inner fortitude.

What could possibly be bad about that? In principle, nothing. The heart of a typical encourager is certainly in the right place. However, in practice something subtle happens. Most typical encouragement is directed at a specific *outcome*. A common example of this in business is the manager who begins a weekly sales meeting by going over sales goals, then giving the sales team a motivational talk to reach their goals. The point of this well-intentioned (and common) exercise is to focus the sales force on an outcome: sales numbers.

This tendency is common in many areas of life. For example, there is a tendency to apply encouragement to:

- *A faltering internal sense of value:* "C'mon, Johnny, you're a great salesman! These customers love you. Just get on the phone and make it happen!"

- *A lack of confidence:* "Forget about that last call, Johnny, and stop sweating! That guy was jerk!"

- *A feeling of inability:* "I know you don't think you can do this, Johnny, but you've got skills. Just use them!"

- *A deflated self-image:* "I know that client thinks you're a total idiot, Johnny, but you're a great guy no matter what anyone says."

We tend to hear and use encouragement as an ego boost to achieve an outcome like a sale, more production, a better score, more touchdowns, or some other objective.

In almost every case, this form of encouragement creates internal pressure that heightens anxiety and degrades performance. Psychologically, this type of encouragement focuses people's attention on things they cannot control directly. That is, they cannot control the outcome of a game or a sales call. There are just too many variables involved that are out of their personal control. Subconsciously they know they can't control the outcome, and the lack of control creates distress and distraction.

There must be a better way than this typical form of encouragement.

Encouragement as a Process Reminder

A more effective way to encourage people is to *remind* them to focus on their process and forget about the outcome. This is a huge, empowering distinction. Be clear about the difference: Typical encouragement points people toward an *outcome*, but supereffective encouragement points them toward a *process*.

Why is pointing back to the *process* better than pointing at the outcome? Two reasons: First, an outcome is only something you can observe, whereas a process is something you can do. A process encouragement is not an opinion or a judgment of yourself, nor is it a reference to any activity going on outside yourself, like in outcome-based encouragement. It is also not a feeling like, "Cheer up, Johnny! You can do this! Just think about how good it feels to make a sale!" This common form of outcome encouragement, rather than causing higher levels of performance, prompts people to think too much about things they cannot control. When they do this, they put their self-worth on the line, in essence saying to themselves, "If I don't make this happen, I'm dirt." Psychologically speaking, if the outcome turns out bad (for example, you lose the game or don't get the A), you will actually feel worth *less*.

Everyone has experienced getting their armor chinked because they lost at something they should have won. When the focus of encouragement is on your making something happen in a situation where you have no real control, the chance of failure is huge. It's a very human thing to take such a loss or failure personally and to think less of yourself as a result. Rather than feeling responsibility over an error ("I failed"), you feel a sense of shame ("I am a failure").

According to the social learning theories of Julian Rodder, 78 percent of people admit to allowing forces and situations *outside* themselves to control how they feel about themselves on the *inside*. In other words, 78 percent of people are focusing on the scoreboard of life rather than on their process. This is destructive to self-worth and productivity because people with degraded self-worth act differently from those who feel they have value. Their low self-worth shows up in struggle and strain to meet an outcome driven by a need to justify themselves and to feel OK.

They stress out, get angry, blow up easily, get entangled in anxiety, and feel pressured because so much of their value is on the line. Attaching your self-worth to an outcome is a very difficult, tension-laden, and struggle-filled way to live. Nobody can attain a position of life-satisfying greatness if they're clogged by a sense of shame and worthlessness. In fact, if that is your state of mind, you can expect to act in ways that focus on immediate gratification instead of working a long-term vision. This is the reason, in our opinion, why, according to T. Harv Eker in his book *Secrets of the Millionaire Mind, only 4 percent of NFL players retire as millionaires.* The vast majority of the players are broke within two years, having lost their money through excessive spending, ill-conceived financial schemes, partying, and other external attempts to bolster their financial standing or sense of worth.

Attaching your valuable self-worth to a *process* rather than to an *outcome* sidesteps all these problems. Attaching your worth to a process (like the one we created in the last chapter) allows you psychologically to keep their self-worth out of the equation, to feel good about yourself, to play harder, to work harder, to love more, and to give more. Attaching yourself to a doable and dynamic internal process rather than an external standard is transforming.

I, Bill, once worked with a promising corporate vice president who was suffering burnout from competition and the rigors of coaxing his team to making its sales numbers. After spending some time hearing his situation, it became clear that the reason he was suffering burnout had really nothing to do with his work.

Rather it was all related to the fact that he was in a constant state of self-condemnation because his team's sales numbers had been slowly declining, and he was in danger of not making his quota and potentially losing his job. His entire sense of worth was tied to an outcome: money. The standard of success was totally external.

I addressed this problem by asking him to focus not on his team's sales figures for his sense of worth, but on the process of his daily routine. I made it a point to suggest that he should judge his worth not on the basis of his sales stats, but on whether he made sales-related calls every hour, as hard as he could. If he called hard, he was allowed to feel good about himself. Over the course of weeks, I drilled this new process focus into him so successfully that he began to shift his thinking, allowing himself for the first time in his career to feel good about himself for internal reasons (making success-oriented calls) instead of an external standard (sales numbers). Not only did he feel better, but his sales got significantly better, as did those of his team. He felt relaxed and rejuvenated, and he began really climbing. Not that any of that mattered to him anymore, because in reality it didn't.

The second good reason for using encouragement to point at the process is that so few people are doing it. Process encouragement gives your words freshness and gravity. The newness and uniqueness of process encouragement make your words more effective. Rather than just stroking someone's fragile ego, you are directing attention to a truth valuable for not only success, but for true greatness: *Just do the process and winning will happen.*

Ask yourself the secret of your success.

Listen to your answer and practice it.

RICHARD BACH

A Sports Illustration

The encouragement lesson can be easily illustrated in sports. The goal in sports is simple: getting the high score and winning. The problem is that when you focus on score and the scoreboard, you start doing things that make the job *harder*. You start focusing on external thoughts like whether you can get a touchdown or nail a three-pointer or hit that home run. Focusing on these external measures of success puts self-worth on the line, thus increasing the pressure. "Am I good enough to score?" becomes the most powerful, compelling experience. You start talking to yourself and feeling an enormous burden about whether you are *in fact* good enough. Psychologically, you think about "*being* good enough" instead of "*playing* good enough." Pressure skyrockets, and performance cascades downward under these conditions. Scoring becomes more difficult, and the whole situation becomes pressured, nasty, circular, and self-defeating.

A much more successful strategy for achieving success in sports situations is focusing on process. That means forgetting the scoreboard and doing your job just as well as you can on the next play, working on getting open in three-point territory, and keeping your eye on the ball. It means putting all your focus—all of it—on the specifics of your job. When you focus on your process instead of on the scoreboard, you relax and your attention becomes focused on the things that can make a difference in the outcome.

Focus on the Process and Winning Will Happen

The Pittsburgh Penguins were getting ready to host the LA Kings. The Penguins goalie, Peter Skudra, was not looking forward to the game or playing against the NHL's dominant star of the day, "The Great One," Wayne Gretsky.

"Gretsky's going to be in his office all night," the goalie said over and over before the game. Gretsky was known to sit in the space behind the goal and wait for his chance to score. Players called it his "office."

Skudra wasn't focusing on his process, but on Gretsky. I, Kevin, was working with Pittsburgh at the time and reminded him that his job wasn't to stop Gretsky; his job was to stop the puck. A small focus change, but a powerful focus change. The Penguins won.

The process plays an important role in the road to greatness. A process gives you something to refer to—a road map that's way more useful than subconsciously putting yourself on trial every time you try to do something proactive.

A Note About Encouraging Yourself as Opposed to Encouraging Others

There is no distinction at all between what it takes to properly encourage yourself instead of properly encouraging others. The pattern is the same, the words are the same, and the calling-you-back-to-your-process objective is the same.

Most of us respond to encouragement from time to time. It is a human need, and many of us are looking for someone to believe in us and verbally affirm us. Have you ever wondered why encouragement isn't offered more often? Why aren't co-workers, bosses, teachers, and others more encouraging of one another, instead of being harsh and judgmental? One of the reasons is that people have no idea what to say. Our world is not an encouraging place, so people have had few good examples to model. Encouraging words seem odd and foreign, and there is a general hesitancy to use them.

Another reason general encouragement fails to occur more often is that the encouragement can seem unwelcome. Encouragers are sometimes ridiculed by outsiders as deluded and as "looking through rose-colored glasses." Those who need the encouragement often dismiss the well-intended words as pity. Nobody likes their heartfelt encouragements treated this way and typically make the decision just to say nothing. These pressures and realities conspire to make the outright encouragement of one another a rare event.

That needs to change. The exercise of greatness relies on

reaching out to others. There is no better way to begin to express your own greatness than by offering encouragement to others and by encouraging yourself in ways that cause you to grow and expand. Here are some simple ways to begin offering effective process encouragement to others and yourself.

1. Verbal process encouragement

3. Belief process encouragement

3. Mastermind team process encouragement

4. Surrender and detach process encouragement

1. Verbal Process Encouragement

Verbal process encouragement is what we typically think of when we hear the word "encouragement." It involves saying something soothing or empowering to someone else or yourself. But many of us don't even know what to say in these situations. Here are some very specific examples you can commit to memory and use over and over. These comments are custom designed to direct people back to their inner vision and to get their heads off the scoreboard of life. You can begin using these process encouragements immediately.

- What's your vision?

- Focus on what you have to do.

- Put all your effort into just the next thing you do.

- What is the next thing you can do?

- What's your process for success?

- Relax your mind.

- Keep it simple—just the next thing.

- Just the next step . . .

- Focus on the next step, not clear on down the road.

- Stay in the present.

- Be present.

- Stay absorbed in the moment.

- What one or two things can you do right now?

- Find the best in you and give it right now.

- One step at a time . . .

- What's the next step?

- Control what you can control.

- Focus on what you can do right now.

- Just play the game.

- Play your game, not anyone else's.

- Just show up

- What are you thankful for?

- What's your vision? Don't tell me about how, just your vision.

- Let go.

- Do you believe this can happen? Can you see it happening? See it.

Look carefully at each of these process encouragements. None of them is what you might typically consider to be an encouragement. What they do is direct attention in a different direction and cause hearers to get their heads off pressurizing and confidence-rattling self-talk and onto the kind of thinking that leads toward relaxed focus.

Just notice the difference in saying, "C'mon, Joe! You can do it. You know how to hit that ball! Just give it ride!" instead of "Focus on what you can do: plant your feet, relax your arms, watch the ball, and swing evenly." What you hear is the difference between encouragement and process encouragement.

Another way to utilize verbal process encouragement is to counter the things that others say with process-oriented replies.

They say . . .	You say . . .
"Nothing I'm doing works."	"Stay focused on what you can do."
"I stink."	"What part of this do you do well?"
"I'll never get an A."	"Focus on your preparation for tests."
"We're gonna get killed."	"Trust yourself; take it step by step."
"I stink at sales."	"Focus on the next phone call alone."
"I want to quit."	"Take one new step, right now."

Beware of one thing: People may not get your encouraging them this way. They are used to rah-rah, ego-stroke encouragement and may not understand what you're doing. Though they may not say anything, the encouragement will sound different: not bad, just different. What they may be looking for you to do is to soothe their battered and bruised self-worth with upbeat words. But such standard types of encouragement lead to poor results. Because they only point out that subconsciously standard encouragement, they only make a bad situation worse. If people don't understand your explanation, don't worry about explaining anything. Simply offer process encouragement, and let it do what it does: refocus hearers on what works for superior performance.

Now take this lesson and apply it to your own self-talk: If you have a way of *talking* that degrades how you feel about yourself, rephrase your words so they take you back to your process. Forget saying, "C'mon, Sue, get with it! You can do better than this!" Instead, say, "I am really good at doing this one part of my job, and I'm going to focus on it right now" or "I can't fix this whole problem right now, but I can work on this one step." Notice again that the regular type of encouragement is more like high-volume cheerleading, and process encouragement is more like reminding yourself of the specific two, three, or four steps you need to take to be successful.

Signs and symbols

Verbal process encouragement does not always consist of spoken words. Sometimes the verbal process reminders come in the form of the ubiquitous signs and symbols that fill our lives.

We are surrounded by signs and symbols that have all sorts of "spoken-like" impact on us. Examples range from a company's mission statement posted at the door of work, reminding everyone about the process driving the organization, to a family crest, a list of written quotes that we use to bolster ourselves, St. Christopher statues on the dashboard, crosses, or tattoos. Signs and symbols we use for aligning ourselves are everywhere.

We would strongly advocate that you review all the symbols, sayings, icons, and reminders around you and evaluate their effectiveness in your life. Are they just admonishing you, creating guilt, happiness, power? Or, better yet, do they focus you back onto your process?

When you do this inventory, you may be surprised to find out first how many there are, and second how much impact these physical symbols have on you without your knowledge. For example, you may have a religious symbol or picture that makes you feel guilty, an old set of clothes that makes you feel fat, an object in your house or office that has a bad connotation. Replace the religious symbols and pictures with religious symbols that causes you to feel joy and kindness toward individuals. Replace your clothes with some that make you feel different—powerful, stylish, attractive, credible, sexy, and better in some way. Replace any physical object in your world that makes you feel uncomfortable or bad in some way. Get the symbolism that is supposed to be working for you actually working directly for you by reminding you of your process.

Mantras

Slogans, witty phrases, physical movements, auditory chants, prayers, recordings, and so on are what we'd refer to as mantras. Mantras are words or physical motions you repeat to yourself to keep your mind focused on one small aspect of the process you wish to improve.

Physical mantras focus attention on doable behavior rather than on scores, grades, goals, quotas, and other measures of success. For those of you who like sports, think of the Rutgers' Chop in college football. The motion (a chopping motion made with the hands) suggests that players forget about the score, the last down, the overall situation, and just "chop wood." This simple motions tells players to stay focused on the task at hand on each play. Just take chop after chop, and don't think about the score.

College sports, the military, and other institutions do a great job of reinforcing a collective identity this way. For example, Penn State University routinely chants "We Are Penn State!" This slogan focuses crowds on their collective identity and on their identity and tradition. The same goes with the Florida State tomahawk chop, the "hook 'em horns" finger motion of the University of Texas Longhorns, the "Go Blue" of Michigan, and so on. The U.S. Marines have "Semper fi" and emblaze that mantra into the mind of any person who unites his life with the marines. The Elko family motto is, "We will serve others." These are all examples of simple verbal encouragements (mantras, if you will) that put people back into a process of molding their identity. Encourage those in your immediate world in a similar fashion, taking care to create a mantra if necessary.

Once I, Bill, was speaking to a large gathering of executives of a large insurance company. Needing a new mantra around which to organize their multilayered company, I told the story of the two dogs we all have within ourselves: a red dog and a white dog. The red dog is mean: It yells and complains and generally degrades us and the life we live. The white dog, on the other hand, is an optimistic dog, full of good words, ideas, suggestions, and good cheer. They both exist in our heads and constantly vie for our attention. In fact, they don't just vie for our attention; they fight for it. They fight all morning, all afternoon, and all night—from the time you wake until the time you sleep. The dog who wins, I told the executives, is the dog that gets fed. "Feed the white dog," I admonished. *Feed the white dog.*

A year later I was asked to come back to the company. To my surprise and delight, "Feed the White Dog" had become a company mantra, widely accepted and used by management to focus employees on making sure they feed the white dog within themselves. It's a great example of building a mantra that captures the point of process encouragement.

2. Belief Process Encouragement

Encouraging beliefs in others (and in yourself) is very important. Why? Beliefs are in themselves process activities (when you talk about belief, you are right in the process), and belief is closely tied to passion. For example:

- Do you believe in yourself?

- Do you believe what you are doing can succeed?

- Do you believe that your process is right for what you are doing?

- Can you learn to believe new things and bigger things?

If you look carefully, you'll see that each of these belief encouragements takes listeners right to their process, if they have one. (If they have no process, the belief encouragement won't take them anywhere.) Let me give you an example of how this works in real life. I, Bill, once worked with an Olympic figure skater. She had competed at several Olympics but never really did as well as she would have liked, and she wanted to win. After some conversations with her, it was evident that at her deepest place she did not believe that she could compete and win in the Olympics. What's more, she had no process for believing she could win. We worked steadily for weeks on defining a step-by-step process of believing in herself. When we were done, the mere mention of the questions in the preceding list took her right into her process and ignited a passion, a belief that she really could succeed and win. (She competed and won a bronze medal that year for the Canadian National Team.)

Beliefs and passion are very closely related. The less you be-

lieve in something (or yourself), the more prone you are to drifting into a place of lukewarm enthusiasm and mediocrity. Routine
people thinking routine thoughts have never reached true greatness. Greatness is achieved by people who are committed and
passionately believe something. Encourage people to consider
what they believe and to get that belief clear and compelling.
Call on yourself and others to constantly review and rethink what
you believe is possible. In fact, take it a step further: Force yourself to think of impossible things. Put your mind on generating
new vistas for yourself, and make dreaming big a part of your
whole process.

We are generally poor at this kind of big belief thinking.
Why? For exactly the same reason we focus our thinking on
outcomes and scoreboards instead of on our process: We think
outcomes are what really matters. Our beliefs are not so important.

Our beliefs operate almost invisibly in us, and we rarely take
the time to examine them and focus energy on them. We need
to. In the service of greatness, expanding what you believe is a
requirement. We like this little exchange between Alice and the
Queen in *Alice Through the Looking Glass*:

> "I can't believe it!" says Alice.
>
> "Can't believe it?" the Queen repeats with a sad look on
> her face. "Try again: take a deep breath, close your eyes, and
> believe."
>
> Alice laughs, "It's no good trying. Only fools believe that
> impossible things can happen."

"I think what you need is a little training," answers the Queen. "When I was your age I would practice at least half an hour a day, right after breakfast, I tried very hard to imagine five or six unbelievable things that could cross my path . . . .

. . . and today I see that most of the things I imagined have turned real, I even became a Queen because of that."

Encourage belief. Encourage people to believe more. Focus on that objective.

———⊗———

If you only believe in it until something goes wrong, you never really believed in it in the first place.

PEPPER ROGERS, COLLEGE FOOTBALL COACHING LEGEND

———⊗———

3. Mastermind Process Encouragement

True greatness is an *interpersonal* activity. It always involves the participation of others. Interestingly, there is a mountain of evidence to suggest that human beings are more tightly connected to one another than we would probably believe. For example, a well-reported study by researchers at Harvard Medical School suggests that the number one statistical correlate of an individual's weight is the average of his or her best friends' weights. You stand a 170 percent better chance of losing weight if your friend loses weight too. Our interpersonal connections are subtle and powerful, and we must leverage that strength to our advantage.

The best way to do that is by organizing a group of people to help you stay on process. In other words, select a small group of people you trust and admire, and ask or teach or instruct them on how specifically to help keep you stay in your process.

We call that mastermind team encouragement.

I, Bill, have a very good friend in Australia who has agreed to assume a unique and powerful position in my life. Patrick and I talk often, and his job is to ask me about my vision. He directly and consistently calls me back to my picture by discussing my process (he knows all the steps I use). His encouragement and reminders are powerful for me, and I find them inspiring and motivating. After all, I created them. For yourself, find someone (or five) people like this and give them the assignment of fulfilling this important role in your life.

If you write down a list of the top three to five influential people in your life, several of them would probably not even know they are on the list. They would probably be flattered to know it. And if they are true friends, they would be willing to do anything you ask to help you reach true greatness.

Write the names of five key people you would like to be on your mastermind team:

1. _____

2. _____

3. _____

4. _____

5. _____

Sometime in the next week, let them know that they are on the list, and ask them to do you a favor. Send them a copy of the list of verbal encouragements listed earlier in this chapter, and ask them to use that lingo with you. Explain to them, if necessary, what you are aiming for, mention their value in your life, and invite them to be part of your greatness. And don't be surprised if they ask you for more information or if they ask you to fulfill a teaching or mastermind role for them.

This type of cooperation creates powerful unity, support, and inspiration that *ripples*. In your quest to greatness, never forget the ripples your actions create. It's the theory of the butterfly effect, where a little bit of what you do right here and now translates into major action in others' lives far removed from you.

—⚬⚬⚬—

Do not wait for leaders; do it alone, one on one.

MOTHER TERESA

—⚬⚬⚬—

4. Surrender and Detach Process Encouragement

In my (Kevin's) talks with financial executives, I illustrate this powerful form of process encouragement by using a chair to describe the difficulties of following stock markets. I take a chair and beat it mercilessly up and down around the stage like a bucking bull, to describe how the markets can bounce all over the place, and you have no control over them. Then I suggest that you have two options when the markets are behaving so badly: (1) You can ride the chair like a bull rider and become completely unraveled and disoriented by the violent pitching and banging. (2) You can watch and observe the bouncing chair from the side, from a detached position, refusing to get on the chair and ride it. If you decide to get on the chair, you can expect an exhausting and terrifying experience. All you can do is to endure your beating and hope for things to calm down. If you actually think you can affect the frantic ups and downs by riding the markets (your chair), your self-worth and confidence are going to get badly beaten. You'll end up feeling nothing but exhaustion and defeat. That is because in reality you can do very, very little to influence the markets. Attaching your sense of self-esteem to the unpredictable movement of the chair not only takes you totally out of your process but is a recipe for a stress-filled and impossibly unpredictable career.

A completely different way to experience the crazy movements of the market or life is by surrendering and detaching from the movement and simply observing. Instead of riding the chair like a bull rider, you emotionally detach from the craziness and just watch it. You have surrendered in the sense that you let go of any expectations and pressures on yourself, and you detach your sense of worth from the movement of the chair.

The best way to surrender and detach from an experience where you have no control is to become conscious of your desire to jump in and control outcomes. The surrendering and detaching method is about being conscious of the fights you cannot control and simply allowing yourself the freedom to step back emotionally and releasing yourself from responsibility. In essence you say to yourself (out loud, if necessary), "I cannot control this situation and I refuse to allow my self-esteem to be destroyed by an event I can't control anyway. I surrender my need to control this situation." This is a fundamentally freeing and empowering exercise.

Suggesting to people that they surrender and detach is a very powerful way to encourage them and to get them (and yourself) back into the process. But it has to be learned, sometimes with significant trial and error. The easiest way to get through the learning curve is to start small: practice just watching events like you are watching the news on TV. Just observe and keep your emotions quiet. Then in real-life situations, focus on your process while you surrender to the fact that you can't do a thing about what you are seeing. Keep your emotions quiet and relax.

You can apply this to nearly anything that is out of your control and that might have previously driven you batty:

- Family problems.
- Issues with coworkers.
- Poor work performance.
- Nagging in-laws.
- Impossible expectations from a spouse or boss.
- Challenges of weight loss and health.

- Self-condemnation for mistakes you make.

- Crazy and unpredictable economic conditions.

- Nearly anything.

Just surrender and detach and let it go.

In physics, the second law of thermodynamics suggests that the energy inside a closed system is moving, and its movement causes ordered states to become disordered. This is a great metaphor for life. Sometimes it seems that everything that we've worked so hard to put in order in our lives can unravel with alarming speed. It's as frustrating as it is common.

In the pursuit of true greatness, we have to be alert to our order speeding toward disorder. No matter what you try to accomplish in your life, your efforts will encounter the pressure to disintegrate, and that's alright. Scarcity-minded people frantically fight this disintegration. They thrash and worry and rush around in an effort to keep things together, constantly fighting to maintain what they have because of the scarcity they feel all around them. They become obsessively intense about maintaining the order that they feel they are losing. They constantly fear losing what they have and that things can never be better.

Abundance-minded people do not fight disorder this way. Rather than obsessing about the inevitable decline of the existing order, they *let it go*, knowing that when it comes back it will be in a different and perhaps *higher order* than before. They have the luxury of a belief system—a faith if you will—that allows them to detach from the problem because they know that whatever form it returns in will be an improvement. These people have a relaxed knowing that everything is perfectly on track and on schedule and that our best response to the inevitable challenges and disorderliness of life is to surrender and detach ourselves internally.

———∞———

Don't try to force anything. Let life be a deep let go.
See God opening millions of flowers every day
without forcing a bud.

Bhagwan Rajneesh, Hindu mystic

———∞———

Let's Review

The most powerful encouragements are those that focus us on what you can do: our process. The best encouragement empowers from within. Tremendous life acceleration and inner peace come when you apply your efforts and your mind to proactive action. Giving this kind of encouragement to yourself and others is a major leap forward on the road to greatness. It forms you into a person with a deepened potential to experience true greatness.

CHAPTER 8

Level 4:
Inspiring Yourself and
Inspiring Others

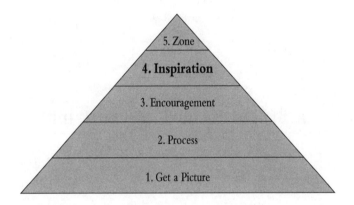

Encouragement is an opportunity to begin stretching out to others and employing the vision-process steps in a new way. In Level 4 of the stepwise path, you will learn about the various options you have for selflessness through inspiring others. Learning to be inspired first and then maintaining that inspiration as it overflows to others is a technique used by great winners. Learning to do this consciously, creatively, and reliably is the aim.

—⚬⚬⚬—

The true worth of a man is not to be found in man himself,
but in the colors and textures that come alive in others.

ALBERT SCHWEITZER

—⚬⚬⚬—

Spread love everywhere you go.
Let no one ever come to you without leaving happier.

MOTHER TERESA

—⚬⚬⚬—

A Breath of Something Divine

The word "inspiration" originally comes from the Greek work
heopneustos, literally "God-breathed." It is appropriate that a
word with such a divine heritage should also be associated with
the process of producing greatness. The two have a lot in
common.

In our system, inspiration differs from encouragement: Encouragement points you back to your *process* (which indirectly
leads back to your passion), but inspiration is about intensifying
and sharing your *passion* directly. Whereas encouragement drives
you back to your process, inspiration is about tapping energy
within yourself and transmitting that energy to those around you.

The effects of that can be mystical. The power is very real.

Think of inspiration as one of the key fruits of your own
pursuit of true greatness. It is something that literally springs from

your personal pursuit of happiness, peace, and contentment. It is the feeling of reaching beyond the just-collecting-things type of life. It is the experience of being fully engaged in life and living on the edge of something you consider important. Inspiration is so important that it is an entire step of the true greatness process. Focus your effort on growing and sharing inspiration.

Where Do You Find Inspiration?

Inspiration is a combination of many things. If you were to take the inner qualities of passion, vision, love, and character, and draw them as circles, they would all overlap at one powerful spot. That one spot is like a radiant power source. We call that spot inspiration.

When combined, these various elements, working together,

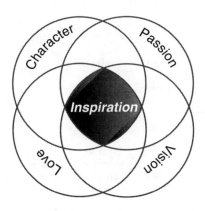

produce something powerful. Their intersection represents a sweet spot of qualities that reveal themselves as personal magnetism, inner comfort, radiant peace, and rippling personal power.

Getting inspiration to rise in you is like writing a song. It starts with one or more things inside you—a feeling, an emotion, an insight, or a thought that seems almost inexpressible. It is probably a combination of feelings, memories, experiences, and yearnings. Through a creative process of swirling all these pieces together in your mind, a seemingly mystical creative process occurs, and you are able to put those yearnings into sounds. It is truly like magic. You experience something deeply personal that you find a new way to communicate to others with music. A deep and urgent *something* inside you is released.

Having the urgent desire to share that something is very human and underlies all art, music, great architecture, writing, and so on. We all have this driving inspiration to some degree or another, and you should consider it a power source that often struggles to radiate from you, particularly when you begin experiencing true greatness.

Unfortunately for most of us, that small and beautiful urge is often lost in the blur of our mechanized, digitized lives. So many of us live deeply simmered in the minutiae of our lives that we neither recognize nor understand what's really inside us, much less know how to release it.

Inspiring others is very different from other kinds of activities because it is so difficult to inspire anyone intentionally. Inspiration is more subtle and usually arises in individuals when they feel something radiated toward them or when they feel something alive within themselves resonating with something alive in someone else. In this way inspiration is social. When it comes upon you or when you feel its presence, you recognize it and know it instantly.

How does that happen? How can you make inspiration a relevant, meaningful, and on-purpose part of your daily experience? How can you learn to radiate it yourself, regularly? Learning how is entering a greatness zone quite unlike anything you have ever felt.

Inspire Yourself, Inspire Others

Finding that inspirational sweet spot in yourself takes some practice. It comes primarily through doing the first two steps (getting a pure picture and creating a process to cycle yourself back to the picture) and then cycling through your process through encouragement (step 3). Spreading it to others (step 4, inspiration) is simply the process of holding the picture in your mind and sharing your energy about what that picture does for you with others. So let's focus on bringing yourself to an inspirational boil and sharing the heat.

———&———

Charisma is the transference of enthusiasm.

RALPH ARCHBOLD, ACTOR, QUOTING BEN FRANKLIN

———&———

Let's start with the idea that you never create something inside yourself (or in another person) that isn't there anyway. The act of inspiration is actually like waking up something that is dormant within you. It is as if we all have piano wires strung to different frequencies waiting to be pinged. When you get near a source of vibration operating at the same frequency as one of your wires, it will vibrate too. If you focus on your picture and use your process, you "vibrate" naturally, and when others with some latent vision similar to yours comes into your presence, they cannot stop themselves from feeling the so-called vibe.

You don't want to take this analogy too far. After all, we are not pianos and we don't literally vibrate this way. But it is an accurate metaphor for how inspiration works. You can ping your own strings, which you do as you hone in on your picture and run your process. You can also inspire others with feelings they can't quite explain but enjoy.

As you radiate your inspiration, you are going to find that your resonance is sometimes met with conscious resistance from others. The reason for this is important. When you get people thinking outside their box, their old rules don't translate very well to the new place. This makes people nervous subconsciously, and they need encouragement to stay with the newness and not retreat to their old patterns of thinking and acting. There is a strong and natural temptation we all feel to retreat toward familiarity, because we can predict our lives better from that spot. It feels safer, and we are wired for safety. This is why people often flee inspiration, even when you broadcast it for free.

Staying safely ensconced in the old patterns is more comfortable than following *another person's* inspiration. That is why the only reliable way to inspire others is to be inspired yourself and to radiate it in all you do. You can't give them your inspiration; you have to help them find their own. No talking is required; let your radiance do the talking.

Radiance, both positive and negative, is going on all the time. For example, do you know people who are just chronically miserable? Do they radiate it? Do you feel the negative energy in their presence? How about people who are happy? Do they radiate it? Can you feel it?

You have an aura like this about yourself even if you aren't even aware of it. Others are aware of it, though; believe it. Hopefully your vibe is a good one, but you should probably not rely on just hope that it's being received that way. Better to position yourself to radiate what you want to radiate, by choice and on purpose.

This all begins when you learn how to be inspired and keep on being inspired, no matter what happens around you. I, Bill, am constantly on the search for people I call "glowers." Glowers have a perpetual shine from within them. You probably know a few of these people because whenever they come to your mind, you instantly feel good. Is that just a coincidence? Probably not: They are actively doing things that create that sort of feeling in others. Do they know they're doing that? *Almost never.* I've interviewed many of the people I consider to be glowers, and when I ask them about this strange impact they have on others, they are always oblivious. They just aren't doing anything on purpose but by their nature focus on good things internally, then naturally radiate that focus toward others.

After studying this within those we know, we've concluded that this sort of radiant power comes when "getting back" from others isn't necessary to fuel you anymore. The only thing that counts is keeping yourself inspired and radiating your inspiration freely toward others.

A radiant power of inspiration is driven by the fact that *giving gets*. Notice the subtle difference: The phrase "give to get" implies that the motivation for giving is getting. Giving is for selfish purposes: "I'll give to you if I'm getting something in return." You're always waiting, expecting something in return for your giving. The second way of thinking is an entire giveaway, without an expectation or the need for anything ever to come back. That attitude that *giving gets* is a kind of selflessness that creates personal power.

One of the best giving-gets is the gift of inspiration, personally motivated and shared through a radiance that you start broadcasting when you are focused inwardly on your process and picture.

This sort of inspiration is learnable, but learning it requires that you have some tools. Here are six tools that you will find useful in radiating inspiration to others:

1. Don't compete, create.

2. Be inspired first, then inspire others.

3. Think of others at all times.

4. Learn to listen.

5. Share what you've got, no expectations.

6. I'll do better than that.

Inspirational Tool 1: Don't Compete, Create

When I, Kevin, was consulting with the Dallas Cowboys, I was standing against a wall with Dave Campo, an assistant coach for the Cowboys at the time. As we stood there, reserve running back Darren Hambric approached and spoke.

"I hated you," he said, "but I don't hate you anymore."

I was pretty shocked and just stood there, mute, not sure what to say.

"I love you now."

Relieved, I asked, "Why?"

"Because Emmitt Smith told me I loved you."

I then approached Emmitt Smith and asked him what was up. Emmitt, the consummate professional, took me aside and in his wonderful manner summed it up for me this way.

"I want him to get better," he said. "I want him to be a great running back."

I was a little confused. "But if he gets better, you lose your job," I replied.

"I don't compete," he continued. "I create. I have a vision

for my life, and what I do is work to create that vision. Part of my vision is that I'm my brother's keeper. It's part of my process. We will all go to championships if we stop competing and start creating."

His attitude—his practice-of-the-process focus on creativity instead of on competition—has become a major cornerstone of our thinking. Competitive greatness is about unity and creativity. This applies to inspiration as well. Stop competing with others and find ways to create.

The world-renowned psychologist Abraham Maslow described two kinds of motivation: deficiency motivation and growth motivation. *Deficiency motivation* is the engine that drives most people's motivation, and it is based on the fear that your natural needs (food, water, respect, and the like) will not be met and that you are never going to have enough. You are motivated to acquire things because resources are limited and precious, and there is only so much of everything to go around. It would be like Emmitt Smith not sharing any helpful ideas with his teammate Darren Hambric because Emmitt feared the lack of a starting spot, carries, touchdowns, endorsements, or money. When you compete from fear of loss, you play with fear and creativity will flee you.

Growth motivation is a mindset that says in essence, "There is plenty here for all of us, so let's get together and creatively find a way to grow together." Growth motivation is the motor behind the prosperity mindset—the openness to ideas (creativity)—and is the ultimate in teamwork. The competition becomes not for who's number one, but for how you can create something massively better for everyone.

The best way to grow is to find something to reach for. *True Greatness* is an excellent place to begin. Once you own this system and it becomes an irreversible part of your psychology, you see others no longer as competitors, but rather as collaborators engaged in a creative process. "Let's find a way" is the dominant theme of true leadership, and you can apply it to anything: marriage, sports, sales, money management, . . . and greatness.

———

People who work together will win,
whether it's against complex football defenses or
problems of modern society.

VINCE LOMBARDI

———

Inspirational Tool 2:
Be Inspired First, Then Inspire Others

You will never inspire until you are first inspired. How do you do this? On this topic Mahatma Gandhi once observed,

> You must be the change you want to see in the world.

There is a famous story about the legendary personal character of Gandhi. A poor woman had traveled with her son many days to see the great wise man. It had been an arduous journey, and when she arrived she went directly to him. When asked what she wanted, she explained to Gandhi that she wanted the great wise leader to tell her son to stop eating sugar because he was diabetic and it would kill him. Gandhi looked at her kindly and then asked her to come back in two weeks.

Disappointed, she left. Two weeks later she repeated the difficult journey, and upon arriving at the place where Gandhi was staying, approached him with the same request. Gandhi gladly complied, taking her son aside and talking to him for some time, deeply impacting the boy.

When they got ready to leave, the woman asked Gandhi a question that had troubled her. "Why did you ask me to return in two weeks when you could easily have told him to stop eating sugar two weeks ago?"

Gandhi was quiet for a moment, then replied, "Because two weeks ago *I* was still eating sugar."

Gandhi knew that true power came in leading the way, but few of us choose to inspire others by leading. We don't think we're up to it. Back in the olden days many of us, including both authors, drove Volkswagens. The old Beetles were fantastic first cars for kids, and though they rarely had heat, they seldom stopped or needed mechanical work. One of the things that always set those cars apart was their reserve gas tank system. Unlike American cars that could just run out of gas, the VWs had a reserve gas tank that would hold a gallon or two of gasoline. In the event you ran out of gas, you could reach over the dash, turn a lever and access the auxiliary fuel tank, just like on an airplane. We both remember using that auxiliary fuel tank many times.

You also have inspiration in reserve, just like that extra gas tank. Yet turning it on appears not to be so easy. After all, if it were, everyone would do it. You will find, however, that by going back to your picture and your process, you tap into a very powerful but latent kind of energy deep within you. You may have to go back to your picture 100 times per day, but if that's what it takes to bring inspiration to you, do it. Focus on living in a place of inspiration and allowing that energy to flow through your actions. Live what you want to see first, and don't tire of patiently following through. Inspiration will manifest itself.

You can assist this if you let one of the main pieces of inspiration intensify within you. Revisit the circles of passion, vision, love, and character earlier in the chapter. When you work on those areas individually, there seems to be a threshold at which inspiration begins to flow out of your life. Take the time throughout the day to focus on your picture or the pieces of it. Grow it, strengthen it, embellish it, and dwell upon it first, then watch it begin to radiate out of your speech, your posture, your eyes, your emotions, and your being.

Inspirational Tool 3: Think of Others at All Times

It would seem to be self-evident that in a system of greatness espousing selflessness, it would be redundant to tell you to think of others even before you think of yourself. But we all need constant reminders of this. Our world has programmed us so thoroughly that looking out for number one has become embedded in our collective core.

In 2006, the Pittsburgh Steelers won the Super Bowl. It was widely known that Jerome Bettis was going to retire after the game, and a Hall of Fame career was going to come to an end with or without a championship ring. Prior to the game, team leader Hines Ward rose to address the team. In essence what he said was, "This is not about your stats or your money or your ego. This game is about helping out a friend and helping him get a ring before he retires." Pittsburgh played a surprisingly inspired game, and Jerome Bettis got his ring.

Thinking of others and putting them ahead of you comprise a theme that always emerges from great people. What you may not have known is that it's also a tremendous source of inspiration, that is, *a significantly powerful way to generate inspiration in yourself if you have none!* It is the ultimate expression of growth motivation. You can apply this everywhere, and for the sake of inspiration and sprinkling its power and effects throughout your life, put others first.

Give everyone more in use value than
you take in cash value.
Then you are adding to the life of the world
by every business transaction.
WALLACE WATTLES, *THE ART OF GETTING RICH*

A sad and poignant story was once told by former U.S. Supreme Court Justice Sandra Day O'Connor. Several years previously, her husband had developed Alzheimer's and had to be put into 24-hour institutional care. While in the facility he developed a platonic affair with another Alzheimer's patient. (Apparently this is quite common because Alzheimer's patients have forgotten nearly everything about who they are.) For most spouses, this would be a catastrophic development, even under these circumstances. But Justice O'Connor is no ordinary woman; not only didn't she get mad, but she put her husband first. She was happy for her husband because for the first time in many years, *he was happy*. And that meant more to her than anything. It's a simple model of selflessness at work.

Inspirational Tool 4: Learn to Listen

Few things will cause inspiration to rise inside others quite like simply listening to them. It is one of the most powerful, subliminal, and underrated forms of inspiration known. It is also the one in which we are all the most deficient.

The reason we are such poor listeners is simple: We are all overly anxious to be heard. We think our diamonds of thought as critical to the conversation. As others are speaking, we are all just waiting for our turn to talk. And when you start talking, others drift off miles away, doing what you did: Crafting their own stories and opinions, waiting to speak them at just the moment you shut up. Nobody is really listening; we are all just waiting for our turn. The effects of this behavior are uniformly negative.

Let us demonstrate a way to listen that is so easy a child could do it. It is also so simple that greatness must be associated with it. When someone speaks, either in response to questions or as they tell you what they think, *repeat exactly what they say.* Don't embellish or add on or qualify the words; just repeat what you hear. If someone says, "I think the mission statement of this place is screwy," reply, "You think the mission statement of this place is screwy." If they say, "Honey, I can't stand it when you leave the toilet seat up," you reply, "You can't stand it when I leave the toilet seat up."

This might sound silly to you, and it will have an awkward feel about it until you get adjusted to it. (We've used this technique for years and are literally never caught in our repeating. It's as if adults are so lost in their own thoughts that they simply appreciate someone who clearly understands.) It will improve your communication by multiples and your ability to inspire others many times over. When you listen to people, you subconsciously honor them; you communicate respect and interest. You boost their self-esteem, you add value to what they are saying, and most of all you give them the relatively rare chance to connect deeply with another human being. Listening is so powerful that an entire branch of psychotherapy was created that did nothing more than train therapists to reflect (repeat what was being said without judgment or comment) and just let people talk.

Get over the discomfort of this. In most cases, people will not even notice your doing it. Instead they will just feel as though they are in the presence of a brilliant and wonderful person. That is how rare it is for people to be heard! There is no doubt that greatness arises in relationships where people feel touched deeply by you, and that feeling begins by listening. Make listening to others part of your process.

Here are some sample questions with which you can practice listening. Just ask someone in your world one of these questions; then when they answer, do your best simply to say back to them what they just said—and watch what happens. This exercise will feel oddly wonderful to you. Try it, for practice, by challenging your mastermind team with four questions:

1. What's your aim [vision, passion, picture] in life?

2. What's the life that, when you look at it, you say, "That's exactly what I'm supposed to do?"

3. What's one personal quality that, if you had it, would change everything for you?

4. What are you working on in your life?

Ask these questions without any purpose or angle in mind, except simply to be a force in someone's life by listening to his or her answer. One thing you can be absolutely certain about: Nobody else is asking these questions. It's a great way to stand alone.

———

They may forget what you say
but they'll never forget how you made them feel.
OG MANDINO

———

Inspirational Tool 5:
Share What You've Got, No Expectations

You would be surprised how just sharing your desire for greatness will inspire others. In many respects all you need to be an inspiration is to start talking about what you see in your vision, begin describing where you are going, and let people be touched just by hearing you. Remember the piano string analogy: When you resonate, others will resonate with you. They want to, they need to, and your inspiration might be the inspiration that sparks an inner fire in someone else. Though they may never say anything about feeling a jolt of inspiration from you, they won't forget it either.

You need to share your visions and gifts, making what you see for yourself come to life in your actions and words, indirectly calling forth greatness in others without any expectations or pressures of any kind. Be your own enthusiasm and let people naturally respond.

Perhaps you've heard of the Pygmalion effect, a psychological effect first noticed among teachers. A teacher was assigned an average class of students and told that the kids were huge *over-achievers* even though they weren't. She taught the class as if they were exceptionally bright, not knowing that they all were academically and behaviorally average. What happened next shocked the psychological community: The class began performing like overachievers! Treating the students like gifted kids made them raise their level of performance.

This is a powerful truth that has been replicated many times. In short, it is now widely accepted that if you expect excellence from people, even if it seems unwarranted, they will rise to it. If you expect greatness from people, they will rise to it as well.

There is a wonderful true story told about George Dantzig, a fledgling student of mathematics at the University of California–Berkeley during the Great Depression. An offer went out to the all the fourth-year advanced mathematics students that whoever scored best on an upcoming test would be offered a job as a teaching assistant, with pay. One student in particular needed the job badly and decided he would win that challenge.

He studied harder than he'd ever studied, and come test day he was ready. Unfortunately he showed up a few minutes late and began on the test immediately. There was a sheet of questions and two equations on the board. He ripped through the questions on the sheet, and just as he was about to begin on the equations on the board, his time ran out. Distraught, he approached the professor and begged him for the chance to do the equations on the board over the weekend. He agreed to give the student till Saturday to complete the task.

On Saturday morning, he submitted his solutions to the equations to his professor.

Several weeks later on a Sunday at 8 a.m., he was awakened by a loud banging at his dorm room door. He opened the door and before him stood his professor, looking rather pale. He invited him in and the professor quickly took a seat. He then proceeded to inform this student that he'd succeeded in doing something never before done in history. The student was stunned: The two equations put on the board were ones that Einstein himself could not solve. The professor merely put them on the board for extra credit! Because he came into the room late for the exam, he did not hear these instructions and had no idea that he should never have been able to figure them out.

He got the teaching position and went on to be a distinguished professor of mathematics at Stanford.

Two lessons here are applicable to corporate life, team building, parenting, marriage, and just about any endeavor where two or more are gathered. First, you are capable of so much more than you think or anyone else thinks. Second, don't ever think that your stretch to greatness—focusing yourself on your task and sharing it with others—will go unrewarded. In fact, just the opposite occurs: People in your life will rise with you.

The key to this is patience and forgetting all your own personal expectations of others or yourself. You can't rush any of this, and you can't demand that people buy into your program. Expecting people to buy into your inspiration—trying to sell it—will dampen the effect. What you can do is patiently show up, day after day, focusing on where you are going, seeing your picture clearly, and sharing it with those who are interested without any expectation that they will join you or follow you in any way. Get your picture and get it pure; get your process, encourage yourself to work your process, give what you have to those in your life without any expectations at all. We like the words of Will Smith in the movie *The Legend of Bagger Vance* where he compares the power of losing your expectations with the game of golf:

Golf is a not a game you win; golf is a game you play.

BAGGER VANCE, *THE LEGEND OF BAGGER VANCE*

Just play your game from your heart, and don't obsess about winning. Just play the game. Your capacity to inspire will skyrocket as you see the simple effects of focusing on your vision and allowing the effects to radiate. This is why it's so vital to get that vision right and go back to it often. Feel your life accelerate when you share your mental picture with others. That's called growth, and not many people get to experience it.

Inspirational Tool 6: I'll Do Better Than That

There was once a great man who lived among the legions of the Roman military. The armies were the lethal arm of Caesar's empire, infamous for their punishing tactics and brutality as much as for their social advancement and governmental organization. The Romans had many devices for using the people they conquered, including what they called the "one mile rule." They could conscript any citizen of the countries they occupied to act as porters and carry their equipment one mile. If the peasants refused, they were to be executed on the spot. The Romans frequently abused this privilege, and many people died at the hands of the centurions for no good reason. The local citizens had a seething hatred for the Romans and their one mile rule.

One day the man was teaching to a gathering of the conquered people. He was telling them about forgiveness, when suddenly someone in the audience rose and shouted, "What about the one mile rule? Shall we forgive that too? Shall we be forgiving about what happens to us if we refuse to cooperate with these tyrants?" The crowd noise rose as his words ignited the incendiary fury of the people.

The prophet rose and, after quieting the crowds, said, "If the Romans ask you to take their equipment one mile, take it two."

The crowd was dead silent.

Such a mindset lies at the heart of a skill we believe is vital in creating inspiration. It is the skill of giving more of yourself than even what you are asked. When someone asks you to do something, your first response is, *"I'll do even better than that."*

This is an amazingly powerful way to think and act.

You might also be inspired by the tale of a young, cancer-stricken boy named Bob, whose mother called him Bobsy. His lifetime dream was to be a firefighter. So when he developed cancer, his mother called a local firehouse and asked the chief whether she could bring Bobsy in for a visit. "No," the chief said, "I'll do better than that. Drop him off in the morning." They arrived first thing in the morning, and the chief told Bobsy's mom to come back later in the day.

That was a day Bobsy would never forget. The chief literally made him a firefighter that day! He wore a suit, got his own hat, and even got to go on four fire runs and steer the fire truck. The chief went way overboard for Bobsy.

Several months later, Bobsy lay dying in the cancer ward of the local hospital. His mother was distraught and thought that maybe the firefighters could cheer up her boy. So she called the chief and asked whether he might be able to stop by. "No," said the chief, "I'll do better than that." He told the mother to go back to the hospital and warn them that soon they would be hearing fire trucks outside the hospital but not to be worried; there was no fire.

A short time later Bobsy and his mom were in his hospital room, and they heard the sirens of approaching fire trucks. The trucks arrived and immediately set up at the base of the hospital by the children's cancer ward. Within moments they had raised the ladder to Bobsy's room. Bobsy stood in awe as he saw the firefighters put the ladder up to his window and began climbing. Soon several firefighters had climbed the ladder and entered Bobsy's room. Once inside they gave him a fire hat, and several fire-fighters sat with him and made it one of the best days of his very young life.

I'll do better than that.

Make this a part of your process and a part of the way you talk.

I'll do better than that.

Can you imagine how life might change if everyone did this?

"Honey, will you clean up the dishes?" "No, I'll do better than that: I'll clean the dishes and the whole kitchen."

"Honey, will you get your homework done?" "No, I'll do better than that: I'll do tonight's homework and my homework for the rest of the week."

"Will you get this report to me in the morning?" "No, I'll get it done tonight. And I will do something else in the morning."

Do the world one better: Be the change you want to see in the world, and inspiration will become your middle name.

Let's Review

The truest blessings in life are to be found in the problems you solve for others. Not to mention, of course, the inspirational impact of actually helping someone navigate toward a better life. Your vision of greatness is good: Give it, preach it, evangelize it, make converts, but, above all, believe it. Practice clearly and succinctly saying what you see in yourself and who you are.

Make sure that when someone asks you where you are going in life you can look them straight in the eye and give the power-laden truth. Then give away, at least once a day, the very thing you are living brightly in your mind. That inspiration radiates.

In this small way you begin the process of making the imagined real. *Very real.* And though you cannot fathom it just yet, that experience is self-rewarding, and will urge you on toward a lifestyle of giving and true greatness.

CHAPTER 9

Level 5: Living in the Selfless Zone

The highest level of greatness is living and working in the true greatness zone, that is, the place of automatic intention. Negatives such as fear, anger, jealousy, back-biting, and frustration are quickly noticed and handled, and acting on greatness in the form of selflessness rules your behavior. The challenge for you will be learning to maintain the changes that permeate this subconscious space.

Review

You've gone through four of five steps:

1. You've developed a picture.

2. You've created a process.

3. You've discussed the proper use of encouragement.

4. You've learned how to use inspiration as a tool.

Now you're at the deepest level, the fifth level: living in the zone. This is the place where you put all the pieces together into a whole picture and learn how to create a zone of selflessness in you and around you, as well as how to stay in that zone despite life converging from all angles to devour your focused intention.

What's a Zone?

A *zone* is the colloquial term for a mental state of high focus (almost like being inside a bubble)—relaxed, masterly, and unconscious. It is most often associated with sports or games, but it can apply in other contexts too. It's the place where you are simply at your mental and physical best at something. All your gifts are fully extended and functional, and you are at a place of supreme confidence and effectiveness at one thing.

If you play sports, you know that the zone is a hard mental state to replicate consistently, and it seems to come and go with frustrating irregularity. This is easily seen in golf. Sometimes you are unconscious about your game and can hit shots with uncanny brilliance, with literally no thought at all. It's easy and natural, relaxed and grooved. Then at other times—most of the time actually—your game is just the opposite: You can't hit squat, and, no matter what you do, you remain tense, distractible, and inconsistent. Same brain, same talent, same experience—totally different game. One game is the zone, the other isn't.

A popular example of this is Tiger Woods. Anyone who follows golf knows of Tiger's legendary ability to be focused and consumed by concentration at a level that is deeper and more commanding than his competitors. He's gifted with not only raw talent, but a studied ability to get his mind in a place of utter focus and immersion in the task at hand. He is the master of the zone.

What can you learn from that example? Let it be this: Tiger Woods is perfectly mortal and normal. But he's learned to combine his natural golf talent with a willingness to focus his mind in order to reach the great plateau he's reached.

Tiger Woods has found his golf zone, and you can find your true greatness zone. Where is that place? It's a mental combination of heightened awareness (steps 1 and 2), focus and ability (steps 3 and 4), all aimed at becoming selfless in the service of others (step 5). And like everything else, this mental combination is your own creation.

You probably live in zone of some kind already. Ask yourself these questions:

- What are you known for?

- When others think of you, what comes to their minds?

- To outsiders, what appears to be your dominating thought or attitude?

People know more about you in five minutes than you know about yourself in a lifetime. That's another way of saying that you occupy a zone of social recognition that is your personal trademark. You may not see it, just as a fish doesn't notice the water around it, but everyone else clearly does. For better or worse, this is the zone you've mastered.

You may want to create a new zone, and you can. Getting that to happen requires that you become a student of the true greatness zone.

What's Different About a True Greatness Zone?

Three things make this greatness mental zone different from, say, a Tiger Woods type of sports zone. First, this greatness zone is easier to get to but harder to hold. When you hit golf balls, you have instant, clear visual feedback of how you did. This feedback combines with an inner competitive urge to do it better the next time. If you love golf, the task of swinging the club and hitting balls draws you in. In the greatness zone, the feedback isn't quite so clear, making it harder to hold yourself in that place of peak performance *unless you are constantly acting on it and getting feedback.*

Second, the true greatness zone is about others and about pursuing your own sense of inner goodness and completeness by making yourself and your talents available in selfless ways. Whereas sports zones are directed at doing an athletic task in a hyperaware, focused state, the greatness zone is about serving others with the same absorption and focus.

Third, the greatness zone is always attached to process. Anyone who has ever experienced an athletic zone will tell you that the zones come and go with puzzling certainty. Sports zones do seem fragile, and they resist efforts to create them on command. The selflessness zone, however, easily responds to a process and is easier to create than the sports zone.

What are the telltales of being in a zone?

- Doing the physical act related to the zone, that is, hitting balls, serving others, whatever the act might be.
- Being physically relaxed.
- Maintaining effortless absorption in your intention.
- A lack of self-awareness.
- A superb, almost beyond-yourself talent.
- A peace that surpasses understanding.

These telltales and the zone they represent appear when you are clear about what you want and you totally own your picture.

When you're doing your genius via a picture, a process, encouragement (pointing back to the process), and opportunities to inspire, the zone will emerge and launch you to a new level of effectiveness.

Why Does Your True Greatness Zone Disappear?

Your true greatness zone may disappear, and why that happens is important. Essentially it occurs because you are allowing *other processes* to combine in your mind along with the process of greatness you created in step 2. The presence of a competing process, especially one that has been practiced more often, can disrupt your ability to operate your business and your life from a position of greatness.

In almost all the cases with which we are familiar, four parallel processes bust up your zone every time.

1. Mental clutter

2. Lack of clarity of intention

3. Working the wrong vision

4. Habituation or boredom

Let's review them, then offer solutions to focus through them.

Zone buster 1: Mental clutter

"Mental clutter" is simply the term we use to describe the excess thoughts you have (usually of a negative nature) that distract you from pursuing "advancing thoughts," as Wallace Wattles might say. Almost every case of mental clutter boils down to the Five Shoulds. These are five irrational beliefs we hold at a subconscious level that drive us to impatience, victimhood, anger, feelings of alienation, and total distraction from our intention. Awareness of the Five Shoulds can be often enough to disable them, but sometimes examining them more closely and proactively letting go of your need to be offended is necessary.

The Five Shoulds are:

1. Everybody and everything *should* be what I think they should be.

2. I *should* always be right.

3. Everyone *should* love me.

4. I *should* never be uncomfortable.

5. My past *should* have never happened to me.

Everybody and everything should be what I think they should be

This Should is first because it's the prime cause of huge distraction and unhappiness. It is, of course, completely irrational: Everybody and everything cannot be who or what you think they should be. Demanding it, either consciously or subconsciously, is a game you don't want to start playing because it guarantees your distraction and clutters up your mind with irresolvable thoughts. People will drive like idiots, fail to extend the simplest kindnesses like holding doors for others, picking up their trash, treating cashiers in stores with disrespect, and so on. This Should will make you furious if you let it, and there is no solution other than just to drop the thought altogether. Nobody and no thing will ever match up to all your expectations.

Rx: Let go of the belief that people and things should be anything. Surrender that thought. Feel the buoyancy of letting go.

I should always be right

This Should is probably more unconscious than the others. You may be the kind of person who when you speak, you expect others to genuflect at your staggering brilliance. But that just doesn't happen very often. Instead you make mistakes in thinking, judgment, evaluation, instinct, and intuition even though you might not see it, much less admit it. In reality, you might make more mistakes in thinking than you would believe. And that's alright. Driving yourself to distraction over being right all the time is silly and constitutes a huge source of mental clutter. It can easily be swept away with just a touch of humility and reality. Release whatever energy you have invested in that way of thinking

Rx: Get comfortable with not always being right.

Everyone should love me

In reality, not only doesn't everyone love you, they don't even think about you! And that's fine. It's always been that way. Being universally loved is a wonderful thing, but it's not real. Jesus Christ couldn't keep 12 people happy! What is real is universally loving *others* no matter how much comes back to you. Adopt that thinking and keep this mental clutter out of your life.

Rx: Let go of the idea that everyone should love you; love them instead.

I should never be uncomfortable

Here's a biggy. If you look at most instances of road rage, assault, marital discord, and other examples of interpersonal strife, it's almost always due to someone creating discomfort in another person. People resent being made to feel uncomfortable because we feel that deep down *we should never be uncomfortable.* On the surface that sounds totally irrational, but we all operate from that place from time to time. The ongoing mental clutter proliferating from this misguided belief is unnecessary.

Rx: Let go of your need to be comfortable.

My past should have never happened to me

In our highly therapized world, there is a strong and lingering belief that past events correlate to our current and future lives. This is especially true if things don't go right for us. We can easily begin to find reasons and excuses for our current dilemmas in the past. This Should creates massive internal clutter.

Nelson Mandela's political dissent caused him to be jailed for most of his life in his native South Africa. He then rose to become the country's first black prime minister, an act of political courage and focus that defied explanation. He was noted for always living forward—"living from imagination," as he liked to say—and completely forgiving the outrageous wrongs that were forced on him. He also made this statement, which we find both brilliant and useful:

> Living from the past is like digging dirt from behind you and throwing it forward into your path.

It is far more rational to think that the past is whatever it was, the present is what it is, but the future is where a new life happens. Maybe your past shouldn't have happened to you, but that has no logical bearing on where you are going and where you'll end up. So stop complaining about it. Work on the next step.

Rx: Keep your attention focused on where life action happens: *now.*

Zone Buster 2:
Lack of Clarity of Intention

We can't begin to stress enough what a problem lack of clarity can create. In almost every case of zone breakdown, losing your clarity of purpose is the leading culprit. This is an easy problem to fix once you're aware of it.

Keep in mind that our minds drift incessantly. Our minds are like children with ADHD: Without supervision and some externally imposed discipline, our minds move all over the place, lured most often by interesting curiosities in our world. Over time, mind drift becomes a habit that is a persistent threat to the clarity of your intent.

A new ability to focus will begin appearing in your life as you practice your five-step path, but learn to ask yourself a conscious question:

> Is what I'm about to do a step toward my intention or a step away?

This question is the absolute acid test for whether you are going to stay in the greatness zone or bust it.

Zone Buster 3: Working the Wrong Vision

This zone buster might surprise you. A disturbingly large number of people are living in a vision that they never considered, much less chose. Working the wrong vision is an enormous cause of zone busting.

You can't maintain a zone for something about which you are lukewarm. And many try! To repeat: If your vision, your picture, and your intention don't reach down and touch you in the deepest part of your soul, you've got the wrong one. Go back and find the right one. It's your life and you only get one! Do it right. Take as much time as you need.

Too many of us are on a path in life (vocationally, personally, spiritually, and in other ways) that was chosen by someone else. Or perhaps it was chosen by us at the encouragement of another (teacher, parent, grandparent, religious advisor) who, in their zeal to be helpful, felt it was their job to encourage you to make a hard-and-fast decision about what to do with your life. It might also be the case that you chose a path at a different period in your life, and in the meantime your priorities and desires have changed. Though laudable and wonderful, you may have taken off down a path in life that had nothing to do with who you really are.

Any one of those life paths might have been chosen without first taking time to determine the biggest part of your inner passion. This is very common. Now just for the record, don't run off and quit your job and make huge changes in an attempt to fix this! Many people have actually quit their jobs and abandoned important responsibilities, but doing that doesn't usually work out. Do not abandon your responsibilities! If you feel that urge, remain calm and follow the five steps. Do each of them patiently, earnestly, and consistently. Discover who you really are by searching yourself, not blindly changing your external circumstances. That is how you find what's at your deepest core, without negatively impacting the vital people in your life.

Zone Buster 4:
Habituation or Boredom

We all get bored with things, and we are all prone to suffer with boredom's cousin, habituation (that is, being exposed to something for so long that you stop noticing it). Both of these processes are normal and probably built into us for some good reason.

The reality is that these are both extreme zone busters and must be handled.

Johnny Majors, former head football coach at the University of Pittsburgh, once told his team, "If there is not a crisis here, I'm going to create one." His point for saying this was not to incite trouble but rather to keep the pot boiling under his team. Intuitively he knew that boredom and habituation can make players' attention drift and their zone of peak performance disappear. What he was suggesting is that you refresh your intention and mental picture from time to time and always be alert for newer and better ways to see your intention.

There are so many places this advice comes into play. For example, the number one factor in the deterioration of teamwork is the *avoidance of conflict*. Think about how this works: rather than flexing and growing as a single, unified organism, people shut up and shut down, and growth stops. Conflict and speaking your mind in a group are vital for growth. If you squelch that honest give-and-take, the organism is going to die.

The same principle appears to work in marriage. Anyone who is married understands that the relationship will deteriorate if it's not actively tended. In a marriage, you either find a way to grow or you will find a way to bicker and fight. Rather than sweeping differences under the rug, keep them up front where they can be discussed and handled. Healthy conflict (conflict that is kept upfront, discussed, worked through, and solved) keeps everyone on his or her toes.

Using the mindset of attacking habituation and boredom deliberately keeps your mind on your vision. This keeps your intention mentally bubbling. Because your intention is the strongest part of your psychological makeup, revisit it often with fresh eyes, and breath life into it by churning it and mentally quizzing yourself. It is much more difficult to lose something you're tending to than something you are allowing to just run on in your head without much active attention.

Creating the Zone

The essence of my philosophy
is that a person should live that their happiness
shall depend as little as possible on external things.
EPICTETUS

You can learn a lot by observing people who are able to keep themselves in their own zone of peace, happiness, and power. As it turns out, maintaining true greatness is about clearing a space in your mind, especially for selflessness. Clearing this space happens when you hold simple thought keys in mind at the same time. The blend of keys, applied to the best of your ability at the same time, creates a very different kind of mental zone, empowering everything else you've been working on up to this point. Here are the thought keys:

1. Find your one thing.

2. Dwell on the present.

3. Stare at your picture until you see opportunities.

4. Kill all negativity with kindness.

5. What do you do when nothing is working?

1. Find your one thing

By the turn of the 20th century, one of the most famous and successful Christian evangelists of all time was a Chicago shoe salesman by the name of D. L. Moody. He was known worldwide for his ability to communicate a clear, compelling message of Christianity, and he was focused entirely on speaking publicly. When asked by a newspaper reporter about the source of his phenomenal success, Moody replied by holding up one finger and saying: "This *one thing I do*, and not these things I dabble in" (referring to other distractions such as writing, business ventures, starting schools, and so on).

Finding the zone is making true greatness your one thing. In much the same way as the creation of a process (Chapter 6) is about the elimination of options, the zone is about the elimination of *distractions*. This is a learned habit. And the speed at which you pick up this habit is governed almost exclusively by the strength of your picture. The stronger, clearer, and more compelling your picture, the stronger your ability will be to get and keep yourself in the zone.

Whenever you talk to people who are driven and passionate, their picture is extremely clear and energizing to them. So amp up your picture, and be tireless in making it internally clear and compelling. The clearer it is, the more you will be automatically drawn to it, consumed by it, and in the zone. That's the power of your vision, your one thing, driving you from the inside out.

2. Dwell on the present

Another quality of zone pros is that they don't spend a lot of time dwelling on the future or the past. Why? Among other reasons, your zone can't exist outside the now time frame. Keep your thinking within plus or minus 2 seconds of right now. That short span goes by other names (awareness, presence, the here and now, the present moment, among others), but they all mean the same thing: Keep your mind focused on what's going on right now. And relax: Staying in the present without resistance is a good way to think of it. Staying within a few seconds of right now, calmly, is the second part of the recipe for an emerging zone.

In mastering the present you'll begin to notice things changing. The first place those changes will show themselves is in your sense of clarity as you deal with others one-on-one. You'll feel purpose driven in a sense, more focused than when conducting your interactions in the normal automatic way. You'll also notice yourself being more absorbed in the human transaction, more fixed on serving than getting, and much quieter inside yourself. as you talk less to yourself and notice the nuances of the conversations more.

You may find that you can't force any of this to happen; all you can do is practice the first four steps of true greatness, stay in the moment, and provide a space for greatness to show up. And it will show up in the most surprising and sometimes unexpected ways. For example, you may suddenly, inexplicably feel a sense of purpose and focus. You may suddenly be aware that people are treating you differently, and you like it. You may feel more and more moments of peace and comfort. Being in the true greatness zone can bring many deep and satisfying surprises such as these.

3. Stare at your picture until you see opportunities

A young assistant once entered the studio of the famed sculptor Michelangelo. The great master was sitting, staring at a huge block of marble. He'd been there for a long time, just staring.

"What are you doing, master?" the young assistant asked after standing by his side for bit.

"I'm working," replied the great artist.

Taking the time to stare at your picture until you see a new opportunity is a very good and necessary thing, but something we badly devalue. Most of us do way too little of it. What's saddest is that it is within those staring moments that your greatest revelations occur. All the best things in life seem to happen in moments: Moments of insight, moments of revelation, moments of inspiration, and so on. As Kevin's mom used to say about these inspirational moments in life, "It happens over a long period of time, all of a sudden." Yet we make so little room for those moments because we are moving so fast and not spending any time just staring at our picture, our intention. It seems to be a waste of time. Fight this: Stare at your picture and heed the experience of no less a genius than Albert Einstein:

> The intellect has little to do with the road to discovery. There comes a leap in consciousness, call it intuition or what you will and the solution comes to you, and you don't know how or why.

4. Kill all negativity with kindness

As you focus on your one thing and stay present in the moment, staring at your picture for opportunities, you develop a flow. You find it easier and easier to find your zone and stay within it. That happens due to experience and the simple fact that you're becoming skilled at recognizing it.

But this is the point where you may begin running into internal and external *negatives* that may throw you out of the greatness zone. These can be the negative comments of others, setbacks, moments of being misunderstood, personal attacks on you, work-related problems, and so on. In those moments of distraction, focus on one rule: Kill all the negatives with overwhelming kindness.

———

Quit thinking that you must halt before the barrier
of inner negativity. You need not.
You can crash through . . . whatever you see
as a negative state,
that is where we can destroy it.

VERNON HOWARD, WRITER

———

This is a wonderful time to remember the conflict between scarcity and abundance thinking. Abundance thinking allows you to give kindness from a bottomless well. It allows you to give to people and love them without even the wisp of a thought that you will ever run dry. Never withhold kindness, generosity, and helpfulness; in the greatness zone you generate more as you go along. This is the right mindset for the onslaught of negatives that will come your way, because they come to everyone.

One way to get your mind geared to abundance, or prosperity, thinking is by embracing *what you have as enough for you.* Think about that: Rather than craving more, learn thankfulness and gratitude for the good things you have right now. They could be such things as time, health, relationships, and outlook. Focus on those things being plenty for reaching your real objective: inner happiness and peace.

Always find good things to dwell on in your mind. Keep your mind focused on the good, the pure, the beautiful, and the great. Take the time to find positive things that others are doing. Focus on their strengths and on verbally encouraging them in their own gifts. Be kind to yourself if you find yourself being filled with negativity. Let your presence be a source of kindness in the world. Be a force for gentle and relaxed resilience, patience, and kindness.

5. What do you do when nothing is working?

In case you don't know, sometimes in life nothing works for you. You will blow up; you'll become frustrated, bewildered, mad at us for writing this book, confused, annoyed, troubled, and angry. That's when you need a bailout plan, consisting of two fail-safe actions you can take when nothing else works in the heat of your life.

1. Coach yourself through the rough time.
2. Start giving.

Coach yourself

The first fail-safe action is to be conscious of literally coaching yourself through the rough time. This involves active self-talk directed at refocusing on your intention and reminding yourself consciously what you are trying to do. It's helpful to know that most crises occur in rather short spans of time (minutes to sometimes an hour or so). Your objective is to keep yourself aligned during the troubled times and focused on your picture as much as you can. Do that with positive self-talk and conscious self-coaching. This is another way of saying, "Get back to your process."

Always allow yourself a moment to stop, reorient yourself, and think. Take as much time as you need to refocus. Go away alone if you must. Ask yourself consciously, "What's my vision? . . . What's my intention? . . . What about me is unchanging? . . . Who am I determined to be no matter what the world throws my way?" These are all reaffirming questions you can use when the predictable problems of life try to drag you off purpose.

Prepare yourself ahead of time for this. Rehearse it actively so that, when the hard times come, you are perfectly prepared. Always remember that great success has always been rehearsed over and over again.

And don't ever be afraid to talk to yourself out loud. Heed this advice: The spoken word always takes command over inner language. Try this experiment: Silently, to yourself, slowly count backwards from ten to one. When you get near halfway, suddenly blurt your name out loud. Go ahead . . . try it.

What happened? You will notice that the word spoken out loud completely drowns out the inner dialogue. The out-loud-spoken word has a power that you can seize for yourself if you are really struggling to keep yourself on your process.

Give

The second fail-safe action is simple: When all else fails, *give*. One of the patterns you will see over and over again is people reverting to a scarcity mentality when they go into periods of great failure. The fear of scarcity causes huge anxiety and manic activity to quickly regain losses or to stew quietly in misery and shame over your situation.

If you find yourself in this situation, you need to release your scarcity thinking, lighten up, and follow this advice:

If you don't like what you're getting, take a look at what you're giving.

Giving—just giving—has power that far exceeds anything else we know. A man once entered a room where the great Mother Teresa was changing the bandages on a leprous old woman who had developed gangrene and who smelled horrifically. The man said simply, "I would not change those bandages for all the money in the world."

"Neither would I," replied Mother Teresa simply.

Mother Teresa understood that real power came when you gave the very thing you yourself might want or need, not for money, fame, or gain, but just to give. You can have that kind of power too.

The impenetrable mystery of giving provides you with an

unworldly power to do amazing things. So use it: When in doubt, find someone to whom you can give something. It is the perfect fallback, fail-safe position. Don't drown in thoughts about anything other than just lifting someone higher than you. Find ways to give. Create ways to give. Make it simple. Make it constant. Make it who you are. Just give and the rest will take care of itself.

CHAPTER 10

Reprogramming Your Subconscious

You are ready for audio files, which you can find at www
.beausay.com or www.drelko.com. Creating your selfless-
ness zone involves the audio training that comes with the
purchase of this book. You now have the required knowl-
edge to properly use the information on the audio training
in a new way. You won't be just listening; you will be ab-
sorbing information differently than when you started
reading this book.

The audio training is broken down into 31 short, dis-
crete audio presentations that drive the teachings of this
book into the subconscious. The lessons will be upbeat
and designed to be listened to and reviewed daily, in
the morning, with one idea to be consciously practiced
throughout that day.

—⚬⚬⚬—

If I don't practice for a day I notice.
If I don't practice for two days my wife notices.
If I don't practice for three days the whole world notices.

VLADIMIR HOROWITZ, PIANIST

—⚬⚬⚬—

Life on the bleeding edge of true greatness is dynamic and ever changing. So don't be lulled into thinking that this systematic approach suggests that there is an endpoint. In fact, just the opposite: You will be learning and relearning the lessons of greatness your whole life. All truly great people do. The pursuit of greatness requires caretaking, refreshment, starting, and sometimes restarting. It's the nature of the true greatness experience.

From the beginning, the goal has been to make the five levels of the Greatness Pyramid an unconscious part of your mind. Our intention is to make that a thoughtless, automatic part of who you are. By following along with us in this book, you have laid the groundwork for that transformation.

Nothing you'll find in the audio presentations is new. German writer and philosopher Johann Goethe observed,

> All truly wise thoughts have been thought already thousands of times; but to make them really ours we must think them over again honestly till they take root in our personal expression.

We want these thoughts to take root in your personal expression. For this to happen, we are going to ask that you make a very specific 31-day commitment. Listen to the audio portion, one lesson per day for 31 days. Try to listen to the segments at the same time every day, preferably when it's quiet and you can concentrate on the lessons without being interrupted.

Prepare yourself by getting yourself as relaxed as possible and just letting your mind dwell on the spoken words. These messages are most powerful if you listen to them in a receptive and teachable state. For that reason, it's best if you *do not* listen to these when you're driving.

Listen and absorb. These lessons are worth repeating over and over, so if you miss one or suffer unexpected interruption, listen again.

We also strongly suggest you begin a journal. You can use a simple notebook, as we do, or use something fancier. What's important is that you begin the habit of pooling your random thoughts, memories, and experiences into one place. You will go back to them, you will review them, and you will remember things you learned that you forgot you learned. This is a huge component of the process, and the only way to gain access to that level of learning is by developing the habit of recording your experiences in writing.

Keep your mind fresh by cycling through your journals regularly (every few weeks or months). You will find that the more you pore over something you wrote, the more you wring from it. So don't be bashful about spending a lot of time writing in your journal and reviewing what is there. Anyone who's ever done this reports great diamonds hiding in those scribbles, diamonds that you see only with the perspective of time. We know of no better way to get familiar with yourself.

As we learned several chapters earlier, change happens both instantly and over the course of years. Take the time to listen to these audio presentations at least twice, then again once or twice a year. And watch the magic happen.

CHAPTER 11

Applied Greatness

This book ends with a simple message: Be loving and kind, and seek the peace that surpasses all understanding. Let go of worldly pursuits and stretch for happiness. That is true greatness for business and for life. Inoculate yourself against selfishness before you even start the day by focusing on the new process. Prepare for all that you'll encounter, and develop kindness toward people before you even meet them. The rewards of this will be self-generating and unstoppable. And the joy, peace, and happiness that flow from it creates within you a life that is truly your own, a life far beyond anything you can ever know any other way. This is the kind of greatness that will move you forward in your business and your life. We leave you with a final parting thought of infinite value.

The voyage of discovery is not about
seeing new landscapes,
but about having new eyes.

MARCEL PROUST, FRENCH NOVELIST

The true joy of life is being used for a purpose recognized by yourself as a mighty one . . . being thoroughly worn out before you are thrown to the scrap heap . . . being a force of nature instead of a feverish clod of ailments complaining that the world won't devote itself to making you happy.

GEORGE BERNARD SHAW, BRITISH PLAYWRIGHT

Reaching for *It*

Everyone occupies a certain space in life. It is who you are known as: your attitude, persona, personality, presence, and the like. It's the you whom everyone knows. If you think about it, this space is not here or there, but rather *inside the minds of others*. If you think this statement through, you will see that the space you occupy in the mind of another is to some extent under your control. Your actions determine how someone sees you. If you have the choice about leaving some mark in the mind of another person, do your very best to make it a mark of greatness.

You thus have the opportunity to extend your mark in several real-life areas at work and beyond. You should not think that there are any limits to how much you can mark your world and change it. There are no limits for someone who knows true greatness.

—∞—

Our duty as men and women is to proceed as if limits to
our ability did not exist. We are collaborators in creation.

Pierre Teilhard de Chardin, French archaeologist
and philosopher

—∞—

Let's look at some of these areas and see how greatness can be
used to better the lives of everyone you encounter.

Employee Motivation

If you are a business owner or manager, you know that dealing
with employees is a full-time preoccupation. Keeping them motivated and on task—what they are paid to do—is a full-time job.
Can lessons of greatness be applied in such an environment?

Of course! Despite your best efforts, you should not be at all
surprised that your employees lack motivation because they still
have no clear picture of what you are trying to accomplish. This
might seem insane given the resources you probably invest in
making the objectives clear, including mission statements, outside
consulting, staff development retreats, and so on, but it's true.
For whatever reason, the vast majority of people resist getting
and keeping a clear picture of intention.

This is a superb opportunity in which to apply some of the
work you've done here, particularly as it relates to getting a vision. In reality, you reap a huge benefit by talking incessantly
about vision. It's vital for your people to understand that, unless

the vision is clear and operationalized, everything you do is weakened. *Everything.* Without a crystal clear vision, attention will wander, focus will become blurred, and the primary source of all your team's strength will be sapped, all for nothing.

You can't let that happen. Begin talking about vision with relentless consistency. In a way, it's an act of selflessness. It's a beautiful gift that, though many of your people may not appreciate it, will be a life lesson they will never forget.

I, Bill, consulted with a window replacement company CEO who was a master at this. Christopher consistently spoke to everyone he interacted with about the corporate vision. When he wasn't talking about corporate vision, he'd talk one-on-one to his people about their own personal visions. His manner, his inner direction, his focal purpose all seemed to be to get people thinking. Period.

And if you met Christopher, you realized one clear thing: He was genuinely interested in his people. His concern was noticeable. His employees liked him and worked hard for him because he was interested in what made them tick, and he talked openly about it whenever he could. He seemed to be constantly interpreting what the vision could do for each person individually. They would run through a wall for that guy. His affection for his people communicated a caring that vastly empowered his message.

Making Money

We want to deal head-on with a situation that you may, depending on your mindset, find to be inconsistent: *True greatness is good for the bottom line.* True greatness is profitable. Greatness makes money! The reason is obvious: People like working with those they like, people who value them and who put them first. If you treat people this way as a matter of lifestyle, you will make more sales, negotiate everything easier, generate more and higher-quality referrals, and be highly favored in your business dealings. And this is not pie-in-the-sky: Greatness and selflessness make for good business in four specific areas:

1. Sales.

2. Negotiation.

3. Recruitment.

4. Referrals.

Sales

Sales is the engine of every business. There is some logic to the idea that striving for self-*less*-ness and putting others first is bad for sales. From a consumptive mindset, this advice sounds crazy. But self-*less*-ness is, in fact, good for sales for two primary reasons:

1. The psychology of today's buyer is changing.

2. If you have a sales force, 20 percent of your people are

making the bulk of your sales, which means the system you're now using is not working for 80 percent of your people. You have to get them into the game.

First, the mindset of the buyer is changing. There will always be some human beings who will respond to high-pressure sales (you will always be able to find someone to hammer into a sale), but for many reasons buyers today are far more wary (and laws are more restrictive) of high-pressure sales pitches. This change probably results from too many salespeople trying to sell too many things, to which consumers have become better trained to say no. In addition, people have seen too many scams, have better and ever cheaper options (available from the Internet, store chains like Walmart, and other sources), and have developed a deepening fear, or scarcity, mentality. Consumer and corporate buyers are more and more concerned about money flow. They have their sales pitch radar on, and they steer way clear of heavy-handed sales.

Though there will always be a place for hardball sales presentations, they must be used properly. Anyone in sales knows how delicate this dance must be. The vast majority of people will simply no longer buy if they feel a hard sell coming.

Enter greatness into sales. The best sales experiences involve mutual respect. Something changes when *we know salespeople are looking out for our best interests*. Human beings are very keen observers of one another. Nearly everyone can perceive with great sensitivity the motives of others. Of course, this talent can be fooled, but for the most part we are all pretty good motive detectors. That is why often the best salespeople are the new ones, those who aren't trained and superslick. In these people we feel a sense of safety, a lack of an agenda. Prospective customers simply have a greater comfort and trust in people who appear safe.

Trust. Anyone in sales or the persuasion arts understands the multiplying power of having trust in a relationship. What is trust? Trust is an interpersonal exchange created between two people, built on mutual respect, confidence, comfort, and safety. All these are, in short, the very qualities that emerge when you are acting selflessly with another person.

A selfless salesperson, one who is acting on behalf of the clients at all times will attract great long-term success. This does not mean that you won't be challenged and knocked around like everyone else, but without question, when you are able to engender an atmosphere of complete trust and care, you will make a lot of money.

Second is the 80/20 problem. If you run a sales force, the 20 percent of your salespeople that are making all your money are the bread and butter of your company. Keeping them motivated and moving is a big issue, but they're probably self-starters and will do what they need to do anyway. The other 80 percent are just wasting time and resources. These employees are probably not self-starters and need a push. It is also likely to be true that many of them will just never get with it. Don't concern yourself with them, except to always give them the very best you have. The others, however, are probably lying low, not happy themselves, not finding what they want, troubled as perhaps you were. They will never say so publicly, but that is what they struggle with daily.

On their behalf, take time to be personally encouraging and don't fret about sharing your story publicly. Being real gets respect. Being real touches the untouchable. Being candid and open influences people in more profound and lasting ways. If you practice this as a lifestyle, you will gain more influence, power, and sales.

Negotiation

There is every reason to learn as much about negotiation and to become as skilled at it as possible. We all know that, in many ways, all of sales and business eventually boils down to negotiation, and unlike simple persuasion, this requires some skills and know-how. Learn all you can about the nuts and bolts of negotiation, and when you've become skilled, be selfless. It is a powerful combination.

This is an extremely powerful position from which to conduct your life and your business. Earlier we spoke about the power of creating win–wins. That is the elemental greatness-style negotiation position, and you should pursue that in all your business dealings. To do this requires patience in actively searching for what your negotiation counterpart is seeking. This requires your asking questions, patiently searching, and being creative in finding solutions that may not at first be obvious or that may be somewhat outside the box. Selflessness—true selflessness—will not allow you to rest until a solution has been created that makes everyone involved happy they are dealing with you. Patiently seek this.

Recruitment

Finding great people is a huge part of business success. Although there are a lot of great people out there, how do you find them? Be sure of this: *Greatness recognizes greatness.* Selflessness recognizes selflessness. If you patiently seek out strong people who have a great sense for others, you will have found a treasure. Although skills matter a great deal, it is better to have those with fewer skills if they have the qualities that set truly great people apart. Your business will run more smoothly, sales will climb, and your office culture will improve. You may expect a uniform improvement.

Of course, the operative word is "patience." Great people just don't show up every day. You must patiently begin developing these qualities in your existing staff. Begin living it first yourself, leading the way by modeling. Then begin encouraging it in your people. Walk it, talk it, repeat it, reward it. Do all this patiently, taking weeks, months, or even years, if necessary. Greatness is in everyone, but it must be teased out over time. Use the pattern laid out here as your group manual and greatness GPS.

Referrals

For most businesses, referrals are a main artery for new business. Everyone can do a better job of mining business from those sources. Let us state this plainly: When you have a truly selfless outlook on yourself and your business, you want others involved with what you are doing. Chances are good that you've chosen a satisfying vocation and you believe in it, that you sense what you are doing is good for people, and that you want to share your work with others. This is the perfect recipe for getting and keeping referrals. In fact, when you are really on your picture, you will have succeeded in finding the primary heartbeat ticking within you, and you will attract other great people to you almost as if by magic. Finding people becomes effortless, stress free, and somewhat automatic. This becomes your acid test as to how close you are to your true, genuine calling. If you find getting referrals hard, difficult, straining, and fearful, you're probably doing it from the wrong motive or with the wrong mindset for you. Find the sweet spot of who you are meant to be first, and referrals will flow your way with unparalleled ease.

Too many of us have been trained by misguided, high-pressure people who aren't afraid of acting like jerks for short-term gains. It's easy to think this "style" of business is better than a calmer, more focused and others-oriented approach. Don't be fooled: Selflessness works to get referrals and build a network of loyal, enthusiastic buyers.

Extremely successful and rich businesspeople you meet in life will all bear these truths out. Without question, the most successful people are not the shouting bloodsuckers. The wealthy people may have teeth and be capable of being tough when needed, but they rarely bite anyone. In fact, more often than not, their entire method of operation is win-win, and they are constantly on the search for ways to give more than they get. They don't do this in an effort to get anything other than seeing the reality of their picture transformed into real life. For this reason, they are great lifestyle models.

Follow some simple rules:

- If you want to be special, make others special.
- If you want to be rich, make others rich.
- Whatever you want, give it.

Relationships

Always be kind, for everyone is fighting a hard battle.

PLATO

It's not a far stretch to say that selfishness and unforgiveness lie at the heart of most relationship problems, particularly in marriages and close business partnerships that fail. *Selflessness*, on the flip side, has the energy to change everything.

We both, Kevin and Bill, spent our early years in clinical

practice. That is a great place to cut your teeth and learn what works in relationships and what fails. What we saw firsthand (and in droves) was the effect of living a life soaked in anger, unforgiveness, and demands. Those qualities create a life of squalor and emptiness, and they are caustic to any relationship.

True greatness is custom designed to strengthen the bonds between people. Greatness is about sharing a vision, about having processes that complement one another, about encouraging one another back to his or her process, about inspiring one another on a regular and repeated basis, and about living together in a zone of selflessness. This is perfect for giving to your partner and growing an unusually strong bond.

Parenting

Parent–child relationships are by their nature some of the messiest, most difficult, and yet rewarding relationships possible in life. None of us relates with anyone quite as we do with our kids, and this relationship offers both extraordinary opportunity and extraordinary threats to greatness. The threats are clear to any parent: saying and doing things you regret, poor decisions, words spoken in anger, bad discipline, losing your cool, intense confusion, selfishness with time, and other mistakes. We all know the mistakes we've made.

There are many ways to apply the lessons of this book to parenting. First, be certain to share what you've learned with your kids. They deserve the insight and head start you can now provide. Don't worry about teaching any of this to perfection; just make a start. Take encouragement as an example. Rather than encourage your children in the direction of an outcome (grades, goals, scores, class rank, or other objectives), encourage them back to their process (as a step-by-step system focused not on grades but on activities). Encourage them to study for, say, two hours, focus on being the best they can be, encourage them to think about extras they can employ to improve themselves, and so on. No other parents will be encouraging this kind of focus change.

Second, always be certain to demonstrate acts of greatness in their presence. Let them see it. Do acts of kindness in full view, think of others out loud, give when it might inconvenience you to do so. Having them see it is important for modeling and for setting up an expectation you want them to have for themselves. Talk openly about it, and encourage them to become involved as well.

We are both fathers, and we know that parenting is full of challenges. There is no clear remedy for the whole thing. It often boils down to a lot of work—guesswork, usually—and you do the best you can. Sometimes you do the best you can without any certainty that things will work out. This much we do know: If you provide some of the intangibles you yourself remember wanting as a child, you pretty much can't miss parenting greatness. Generally, kids crave the simplest things like strength, wisdom, kindness, security, patience, and hope. Can you provide those? With some thought you will find that these things are very easy to provide. They are generally the qualities that emerge when you just give some time and attention to your kids.

Creative Problem Solving

In 1927, one of the 20th century's greatest minds was a 32-year-old college dropout, who was bankrupt and living in a rundown Chicago ghetto. He'd just lost his young daughter to complications from polio and spinal meningitis. He felt responsible, which caused him to drink and in time drove him to the brink of suicide. Yet for whatever reason, a shift took place in this young man's mind and he became kinder, he grew more thoughtful, and in countless ways he changed. He decided to try an experiment: *Find out what a single individual can do to contribute to changing the world and benefiting all humanity.*

That was a pretty lofty goal, one that had its roots in a life-changing disaster. That young man went on to become great. His name was Buckminster Fuller. Fuller is widely considered one of the 20th century's true creative geniuses in architecture and engineering, as well as a champion for social causes, a peace activist, and a philosopher.

Many things set Bucky Fuller apart from others of his time. One of the most noticeable was the observation that he had no ego. That was a fancy way of saying that he was not into himself at all, but was meticulously cued in to those around him, constantly aware of how his actions were impacting others, and intensely interested in the greater good. This attitude allowed him to go outside the box creatively, freely admit his failings, and come up with his ever brighter ideas. It was as if, by freeing himself from the constraints of greedy, self-absorbed thinking, he opened himself up to worlds of creativity and possibility. Mentally relaxed and open, his mind was freed to roam. It's a wonderful example of how to instill in yourself a greater sense of creativity and imagination.

Creative problem solving is well served when you free your mind of the constraints of selfishness and let it soar unimpeded. After following the five-step system in this book, you are fully equipped for that new level of creative action: privately, in groups, and in work environments. For example, perhaps the greatest benefit you can be to those at work is to encourage others to free their own minds from the confines of competition, scarcity, turf control, territorial disputes, and other vestiges of a scarcity mindset. Get them to lose their ego and let their minds roam, freed from convention and competition. The ideas any mind can conceive under those circumstances are startling.

Of course, it's important to offer these kinds of suggestions without alienating others or becoming an annoying pest. Do that by offering some ideas and watch how your help is received. And stay focused on your vision.

———

Rules? Hell, there are no rules! We're trying to create
something here!
THOMAS EDISON

———

Leadership Development

One of the hallmarks of greatness is wanting something better for others. It's the willingness to take second place if it means willfully moving others up to first. True leadership development is *wanting* others to be better leaders through you. It's abundance thinking at its finest. Truly great leaders are less interested in gathering and consolidating power than they are concerned with seeing others reach *their* highest potential. True greatness in leadership is nurturing talent in others. In so doing, their own leadership flourishes.

The how-to of this is remarkably simple. Frankly it's showing up, talking about your process steps where it's appropriate, and encouraging people to do the same. In other words, it consists of modeling and encouraging what you wish to create (vision, process, encouragement, inspiration, zone). One thing bears special mention, however: This is one area where unspoken rules in organizations play a huge role. These are the rules that everyone knows but no one ever talks about. These are rules about not ever acting smarter than the boss or not offering suggestions because nobody cares about them anyway. Unspoken rules—perhaps hundreds of them—are everywhere, practically invisible and quietly controlling the behavior of everyone in the organization.

Part of the way these rules stay alive is that they create fear. Nobody wants to violate them due to the vague threat that challenging them will bring about something bad. However, it's been our experience that organizations do not grow unless these rules are openly examined and challenged. Unfortunately, they are mighty; ignoring or violating the conventional unspoken rules of an organization or individual on purpose takes courage. Often the greatest leadership training you can pass along has to do with acting courageously and fearlessly despite unspoken rules that would restrict you. But when you break the rules, leadership happens, paradigms are challenged and changed, and new life emerges from petrified organizations.

Spiritual Awakening

The ideals which have lighted my way, and time after time
have given me new courage to face life cheerfully have
been kindness, beauty, and truth. The trite subjects of
human efforts, possessions, outward success, and luxury
have always seemed to me to be contemptible.

ALBERT EINSTEIN

A strong culture shift is taking place in today's workplace that has nothing to do with making more money and that says something very important about all of us. Employees are seeking a new kind of compensation, and the meaning of it is, in our opinion, profound. In short, they are seeking more control of their time and a more meaningful life-work balance. In other words, true greatness.

For many people today, living a good life comes first, before anything. A study done last year by the popular consumer marketing newsletter *The Yankelovich Monitor* found that nearly half of the workers polled felt they were devoting too little time to "other things in life that really matter." In addition, 28 percent reported that they'd take a pay cut to get more time off. This is a huge shift from just a few years ago and in our opinion reflects a growing, gnawing sense that something vastly more important than money is at stake in life. Workers and people in general seem to consider it worth the effort to discover what it is.

In short, the people of our culture are reexamining their values. We are beginning to show a hunger for beauty, time, truth, and substance. We are rethinking what's really most important to us and in many cases discovering that we've been on the wrong road. What's more, when cultures begin to reexamine what's most important, they invariably drift toward a spiritual awakening.

This is an opportune time for those seeking greatness. What should your role be in all that? We think it's simple: Encourage people toward selflessness at business, at home, and at play.

Get all your passion and energy focused down to one picture: one focused solitary intention. By now your picture assumes a big, colorful, automatic presence in your life. If it has not, go back to step 1 and make that picture as clear as possible. This may be the single most important gift we can give you in this book.

Sometimes we are asked for the ultimate simplification of what we do. Many great people and traditions have answered that question down through time and the responses have been interesting.

- Albert Schweitzer said to have reverence for life.

- Mother Teresa said to love the unlovable.

- Martin Luther King Jr., said to strive for common decency and respect.

- Gandhi said to peacefully stand strong on what you believe.

- Christ said to do unto others as you'd have them do unto you.

- Judaism says that what is hateful to you do not to your fellow man.

- Islam says that no one of you is a believer until he desires for his brother that which he desired for himself.

- Buddha said that the true path in life is to become a fully enlightened being.

- Hindus say to guard the things of others as you guard your own.

- Native Americans say: Let me not criticize another until I have walked a mile in his moccasins.

If we were asked to break down into a simplified form the most central element of what we teach—what we strive for—it would be this: *Learn to forgive and love people.* This might seem like strange advice for a business book, but in reality this is all very good business. The act of forgiveness and learning to do it well are among the most powerful tools you have for the achievement of inner peace and happiness, and thus they are what you can bring to customers and others. They encapsulate the raw energy of true inner peace, releasing your mind from all the elements that distract and destroy it, and sets you on a path of living out greatness in your world.

During the Vietnam War in 1972, a young helicopter pilot by the name of John Plummer was involved in a napalm raid of a small village thought to be harboring Vietcong soldiers who were fighting against the Americans. The village was called Trang Bang. He was told that there were no women and children in the village. The napalm raid was a complete tactical success, but photographers on the ground snapped a photograph that would immortalize the brutality of the conflict: a young 9-year-old girl named Phan Thi Kim, severely burned running naked as plumes of black smoke from her village billowed up behind her.

John Plummer was haunted by the thought of what he'd done. He wanted so badly to find her and ask forgiveness, but he was unsuccessful. His life spiraled downward. He experienced the failure of two marriages and the scourge of alcoholism. But nothing would kill the pain.

Then in what can only be called a miraculous series of events, 24 years later John and a group of several former helicopter pilots visited the Vietnam Memorial on Veterans Day 1996. Many speeches were given that day, including that of a surprise guest: Phan Thi Kim. She introduced herself to the crowd as the girl in the Pulitzer Prize–winning photo. John Plummer's blood went cold. She explained that although she still suffered immensely from her burns, she was not bitter and that she wanted people to know that many others had suffered much more than she had. "Behind that picture of me, thousands and thousands of people . . . died. They lost parts of their bodies. Their whole lives were destroyed, and nobody took their picture."

She went on to say that, although she couldn't change the past, she had forgiven the men who had bombed her village. John Plummer, seizing the opportunity, pushed through the crowds and managed to catch her attention before she was taken away by a police escort. He identified himself as a former pilot in Vietnam and said that he felt responsible for the bombing of her village 24 years before.

"Kim saw my grief, my pain, my sorrow," he said, "and she held out her arms to me and embraced me. All I could say was 'I'm sorry, I'm sorry' over and over again. All the time she was saying, 'It's all right, I forgive you.'"

That forgiveness literally healed John. He subsequently became a successful Methodist pastor and still stays in touch with Kim, now living in Montreal.

Sometimes forgiveness is not earned, but it's simply a gift. And forgiveness has the power to heal wounds that lie far below the surface and that torment people in their deepest parts. What's best, though, are the benefits to those who do the forgiving. You can test the effects of this for yourself: Find a forgiving type of person who's angry, restless, or difficult. Good luck. They just don't exist. Forgiveness has a strange power to alter your life and free you from so many of the troubles afflicting you. It is the ultimate let–go and provides you:

- Freedom from offense

- Freedom from anger over past wrongs

- Freedom from personal slights

- Freedom from festering interpersonal differences

- Freedom from investing energy in high emotion

- Freedom from a million distractions having nothing to do with your intention

Love offers similar benefits as forgiveness. But make no mistake: In any environment (business or otherwise), being outwardly loving and suggesting that others do the same thing may be difficult and extremely inconvenient. Summon the inner courage to do it anyway.

Love has unique power. During the height of the civil rights movement in the South, a young Dr. Martin Luther King Jr. was going to march on Birmingham, Alabama, to protest voting irregularities. Being the proud and honest man he was, he told the authorities his plan. He was warned that if he attempted to lead this march, his people would be shot with fire hoses and, if that didn't stop them, guard dogs would be *released* to attack them and, if that failed to stop them, the police would beat them with clubs. Dr. King replied in a way that would become his legacy:

"You can shoot us with fire hoses, you can release your dogs on us, and you can beat us, but we will still love you."

Dr. King understood the long-term power of love to change things.

Unlike any other time in recent history, we are becoming aware that, when people walk into the workplace, they don't check their hearts at the door. Rather, they bring their entire psychological structure, their spiritual yearnings, and their hopes and dreams. Be thoughtful about that, and understand that in the new millennium the strength of your selflessness may be measured by how sensitive you are to people's growing spiritual awareness.

Don't overthink this. Just notice your options throughout the day and choose forgiveness, kindness, and selflessness, and offer it no matter what comes back. You can either become taken in by the seductive and ever present distractions in your life, or you can stay focused internally, following your path and your picture, and forgiving yourself and others for sloppy mistakes, their inability to grasp and respect what you are doing, and where you are going in your life. Make that choice, and your life will open up like a treasure chest.

———

Do not think that love, in order to be genuine,
has to be extraordinary. What we need is to love
without getting tired.
MOTHER TERESA, *NO GREATER LOVE*

———

The story of the old hymn "Amazing Grace" bears retelling. It was written by a former slave trader, John Newton, and his inspirational revelation that trafficking in kidnapped lives was wrong. He was sailing to the Caribbean at the time, his cargo hold loaded with abducted Africans. Not far from shore and sick with a fever and heavy heart, he had a revelation that what he was doing was terribly wrong. At that point he turned his ship around. The song he wrote is full of thankfulness about forgiveness and the wonder of fresh starts.

The day you turn your ship around is always a good day.

This book is your turnaround. It is the path to a truly uncommon life. We can say that with certainty because it is about discovering and living the life that has been lying deeply in you forever. It doesn't matter what age you are when you uncover this intention, only that you do uncover it.

> The tragedy of life is not that it ends too soon,
> but that we wait too long to begin it.
> W. M. Lewis, physician and writer

You've begun it. Get a picture, get a process, encourage others, be an inspiration, and do it for all your life is worth. Welcome to true greatness.

Index

feelings, operating from, 81– 82
Fiedler, Jay, 42–44
Five Shoulds, 159–162
focusing on yourself first, as tool of
    inspiration, 137–139
forgiveness, 199–202
Franklin, Ben, 14, 131
freedom, 24–25, 202
Freud, Sigmund, 23
Fuller, Buckminster, 194–195

gambler's fallacy, 93–95
Gandhi, Mahatma, 137–138, 199
Gates, Bill, *viii*
Getting a Picture (Level 1 of Great-
    ness Pyramid), 39–71
  and developing your own vision,
      49–60, 67–69
  and discovering your passion,
      60–67
  and having conversations with
      yourself, 46–48
  and power of vision, 42–44
  and sudden changes, 70–71
  and your aims, 44–46
gifts, identifying your, 65–66
giving, 134, 174–175
glowers, 133–134
Goethe, Johann, on thought in per-
    sonal expression, 178
golf, 155–156
greatness, *see* applied greatness; true
    greatness
Greatness Pyramid, 35–38
greatness scripts, 4
Gretzky, Wayne, 108
growth motivation, 136–137, 140

habituation, 165–166
Hambric, Darren, 135–136
Harvard Medical School, 119
Hinduism, 199
Holcomb, Kelly, 51–52

Holt, Tory, 47–48
Horowitz, Vladimir, on persistence of
    practice, 177
Howard, Vernon
  on being on the right road, 71
  on destroying negativity, 171

"I'll do better than that," 147–150
Indianapolis Colts, 81
information overload, 27–28
inner alignment, *see* alignment, of
    conscious and subconscious
    minds
Inspiring Yourself and Others (Level 4
    of Greatness Pyramid), 127–151
  as creative process, 135–137
  finding the "sweet spot" for,
      131–135
  and focusing on yourself first,
      137–139
  and listening, 141–144
  and sharing, 144–147
  and sources of inspiration, 129–131
  and surpassing expectations,
      147–150
  and thinking of others, 139–141
intention, lack of clear, 162–163
intentionality, 26–27, 32–33, 56
internal environments, 20–21, 46
interpersonal activity, 11, 119
Islam, 199
Israel, 14–15

Jagr, Jaromir, 62–63
jealousy, 92
Jesus Christ, 199
Johnson, Samuel, on being reminded
    of truths, 100
journals, 80, 179
Juan, Dr., 82
Judaism, 199